Real World

Colouring Book

For Advanced Users & Adults

50 Images

Created From Real Life Photos
For You To Colour As You Please.

ISBN 978-0-359-82051-1
90000
9 780359 820511

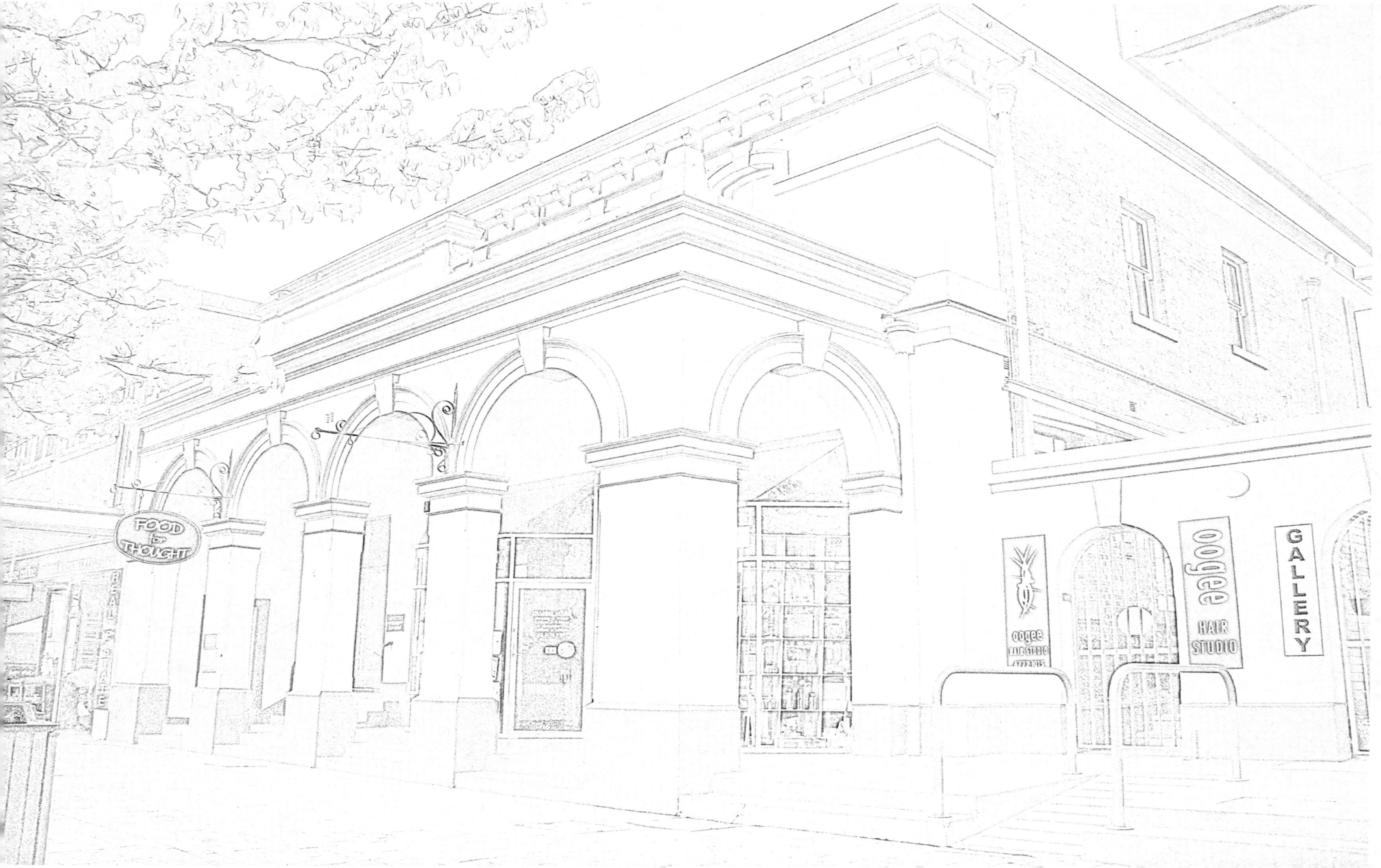
FOOD for THOUGHT
REAL ESTATE
oogee HAIR STUDIO
oogee HAIR STUDIO
GALLERY

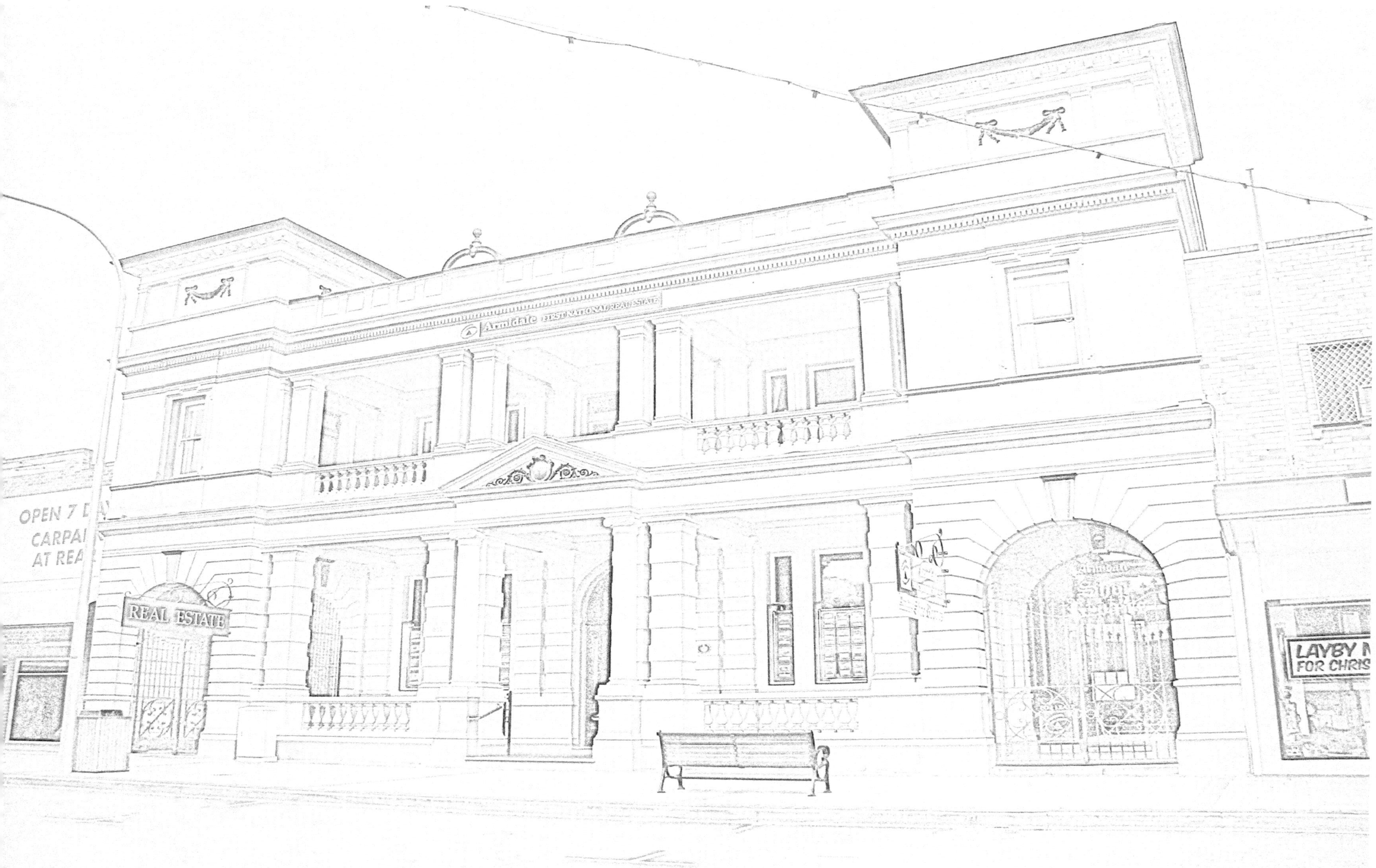
Armidale FIRST NATIONAL REAL ESTATE
REAL ESTATE
LAYBY

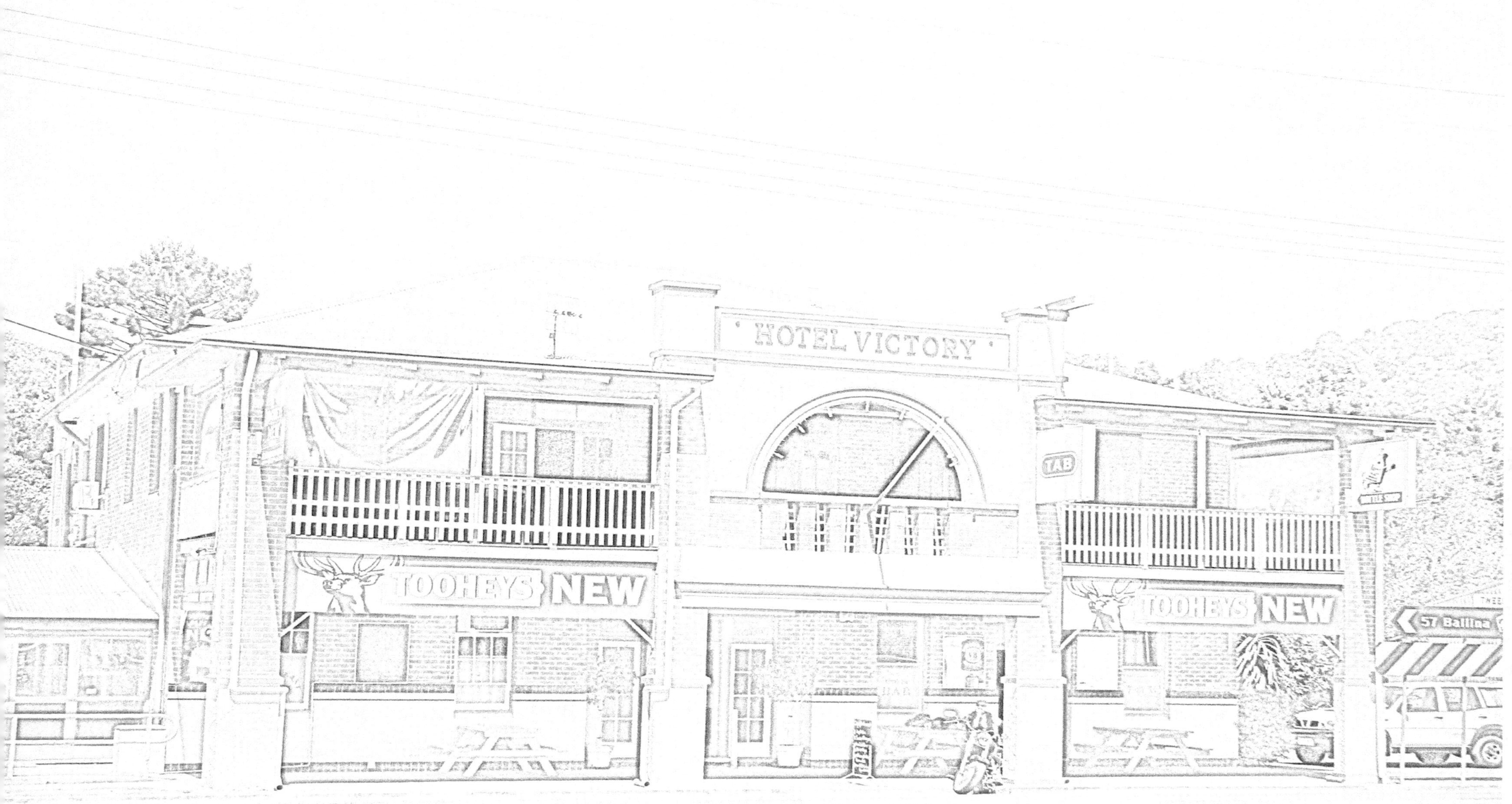
HOTEL VICTORY
TOOHEYS NEW
TOOHEYS NEW
TAB
57 Ballina

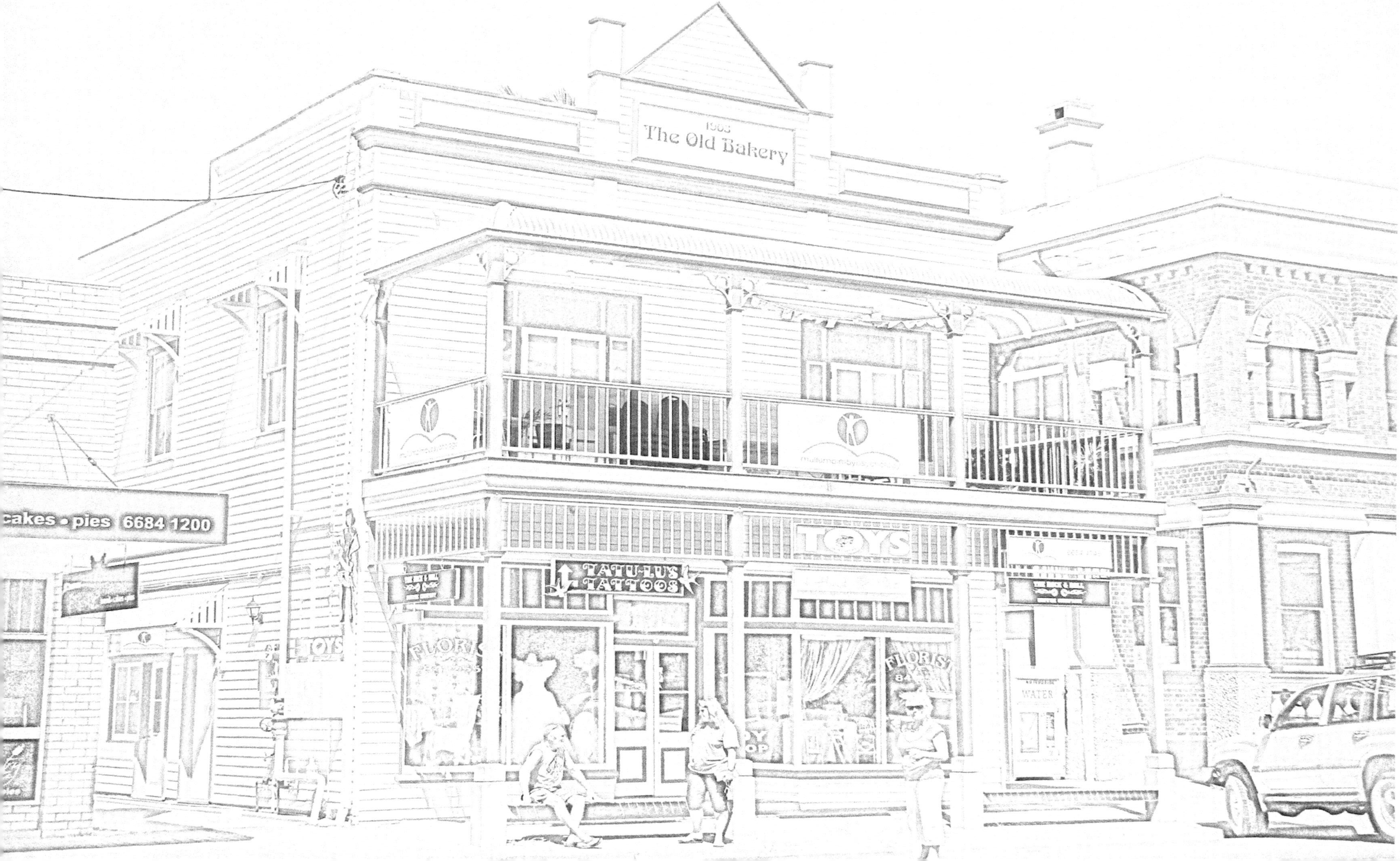
The Old Bakery
cakes • pies 6684 1200
TATU-LU'S TATTOOS
TOYS
WATER

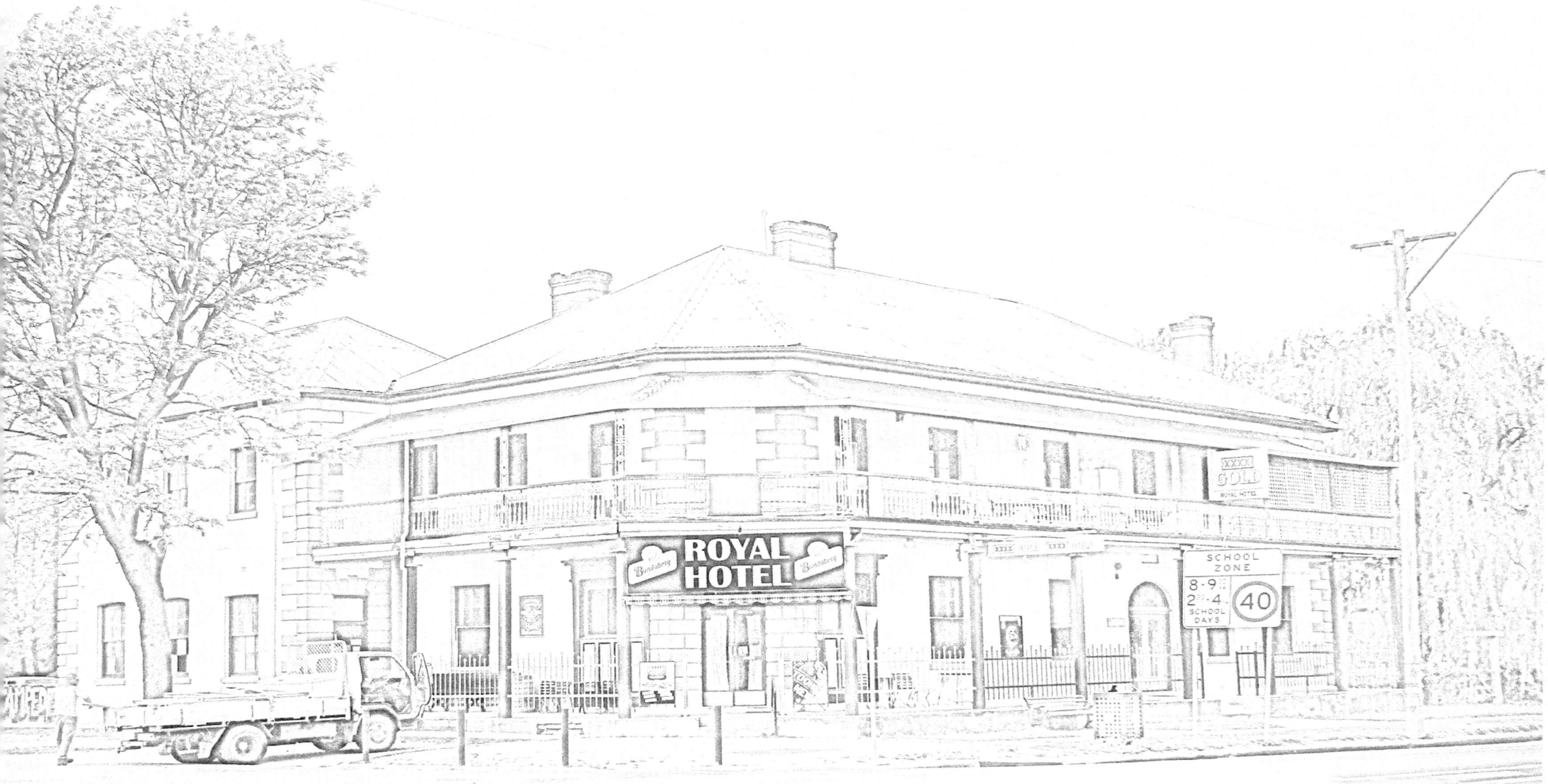
ROYAL HOTEL
Bundaberg
Bundaberg
XXXX GOLD
ROYAL HOTEL
SCHOOL ZONE
8-9
2-4
SCHOOL DAYS
40

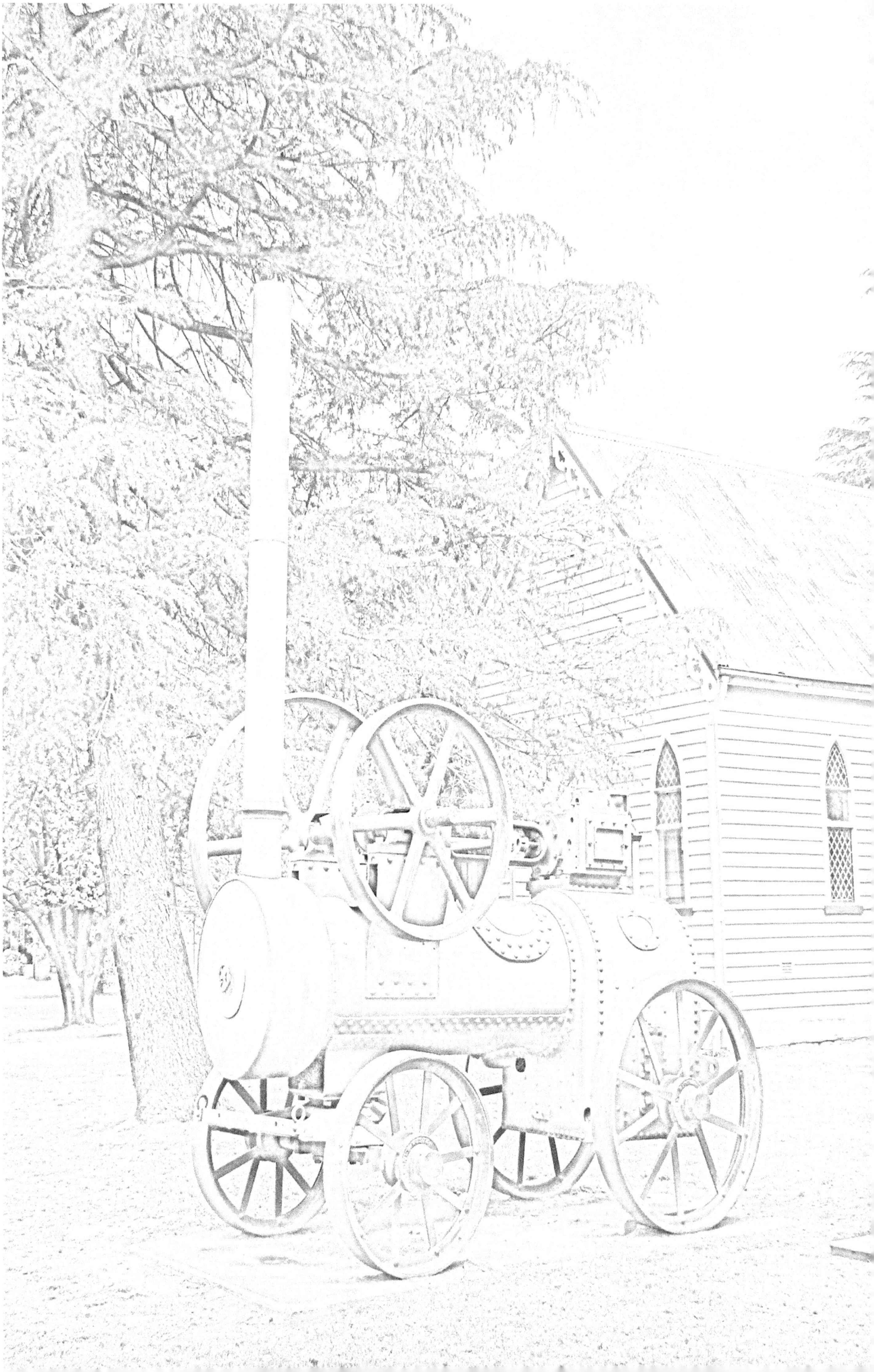

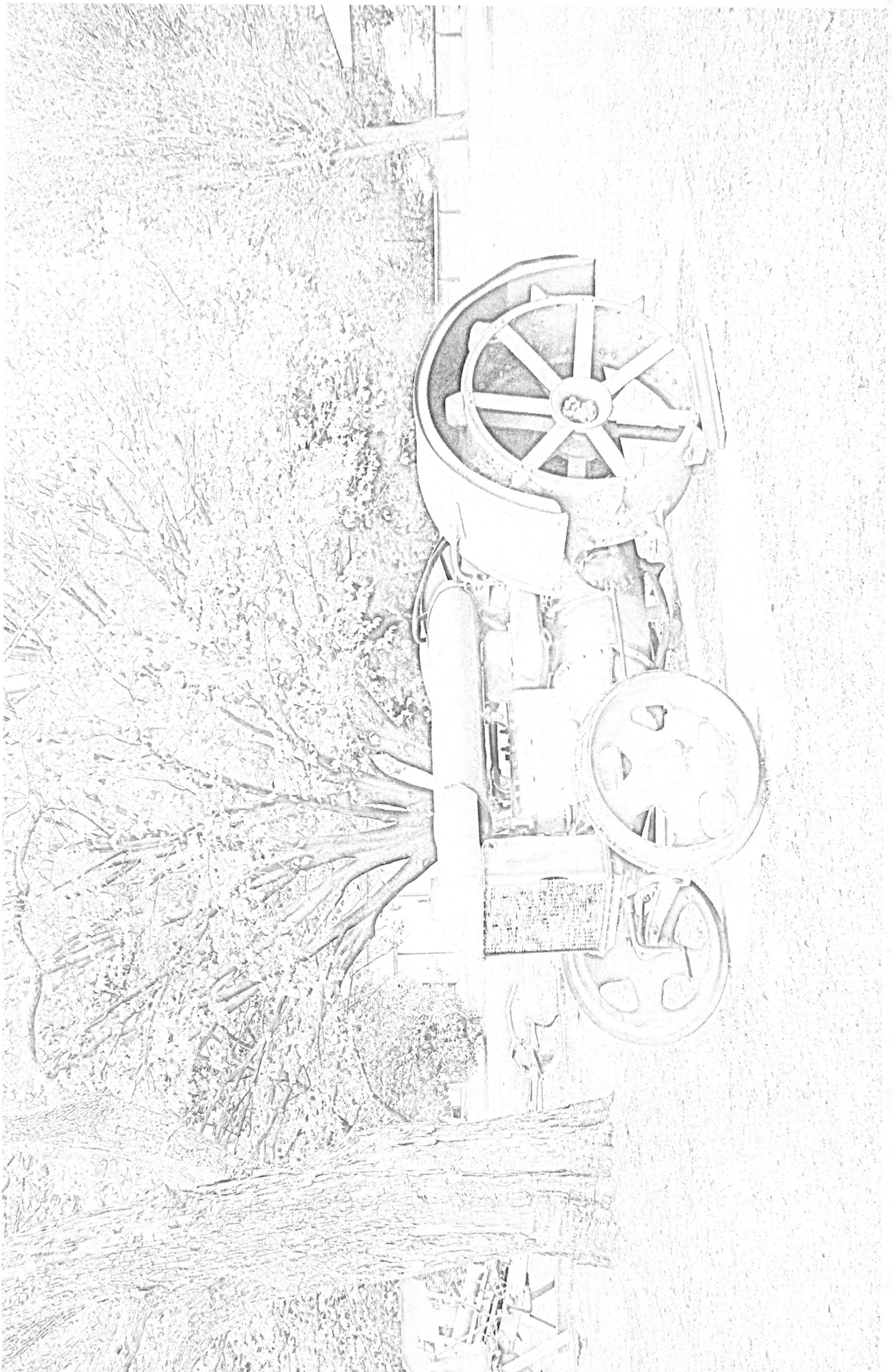

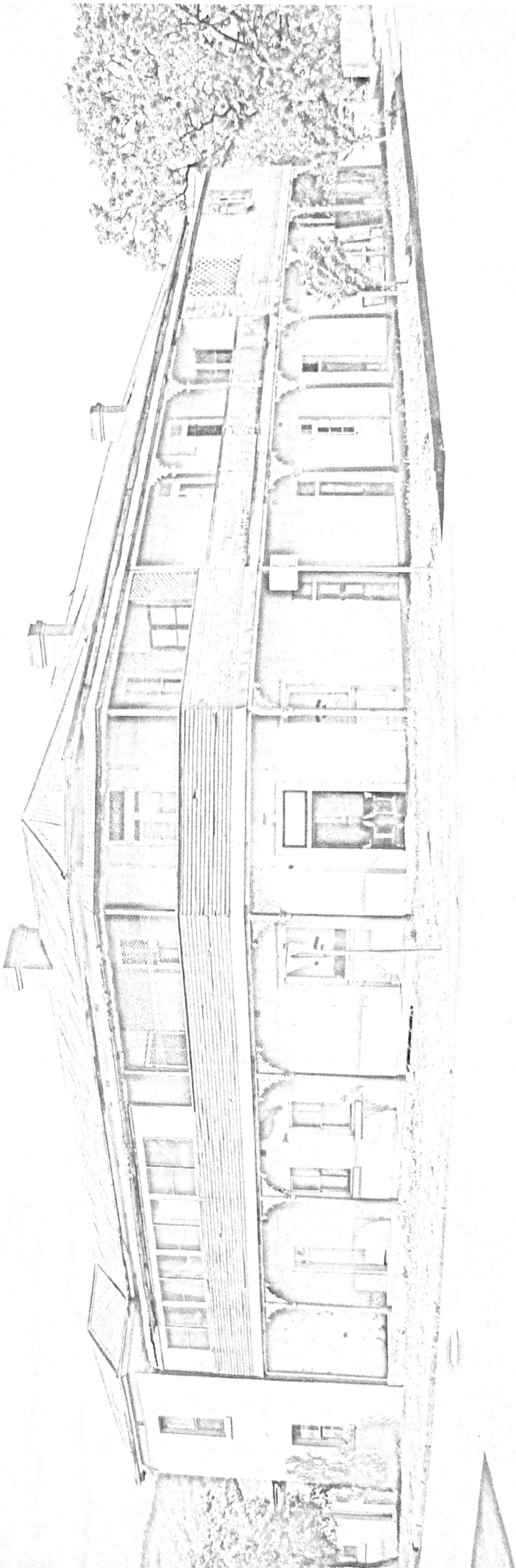

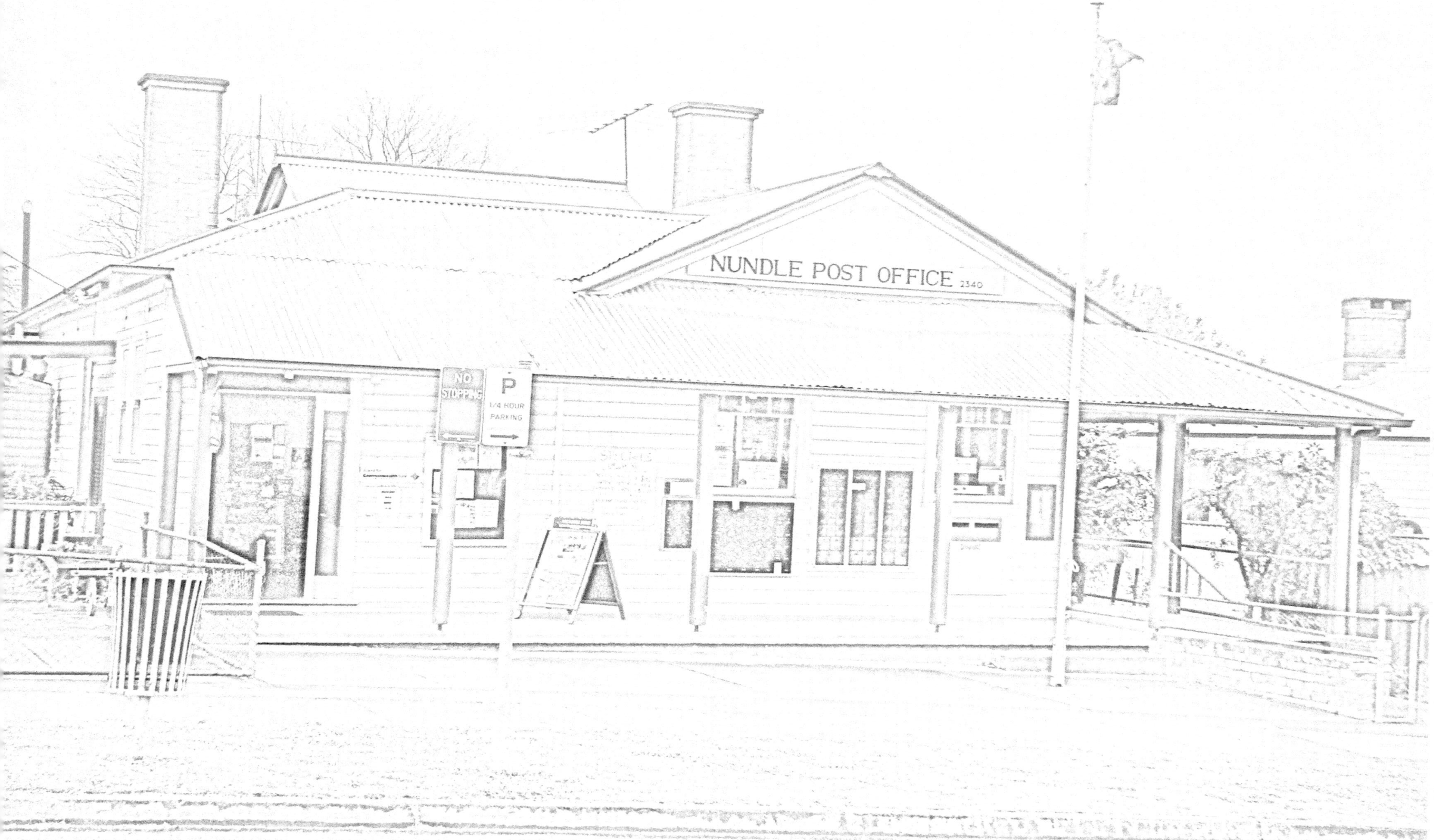
NUNDLE POST OFFICE 2340
NO STOPPING
P
1/4 HOUR PARKING

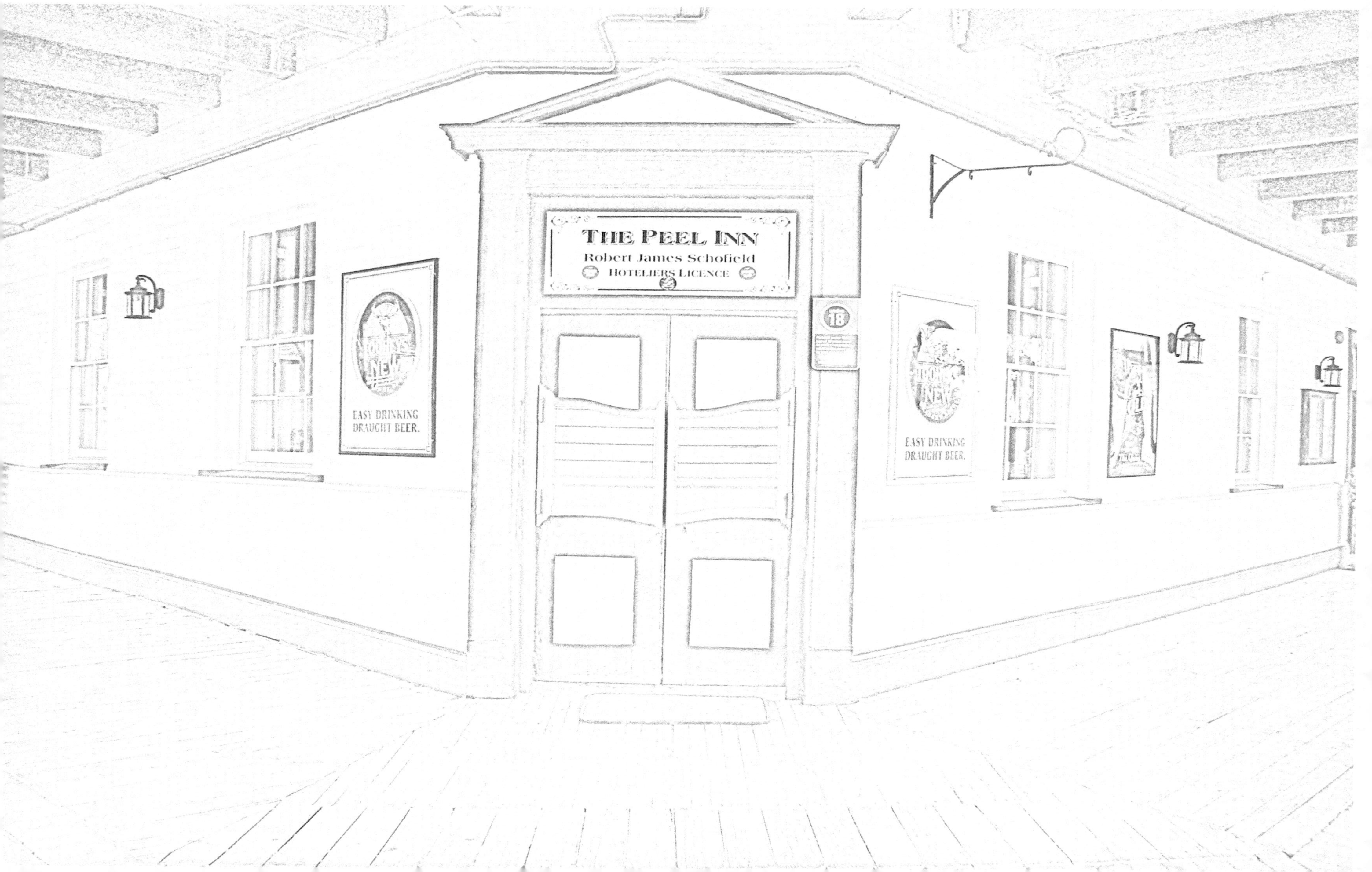
THE PEEL INN
Robert James Schofield
HOTELIERS LICENCE
EASY DRINKING
DRAUGHT BEER.
18
EASY DRINKING
DRAUGHT BEER.

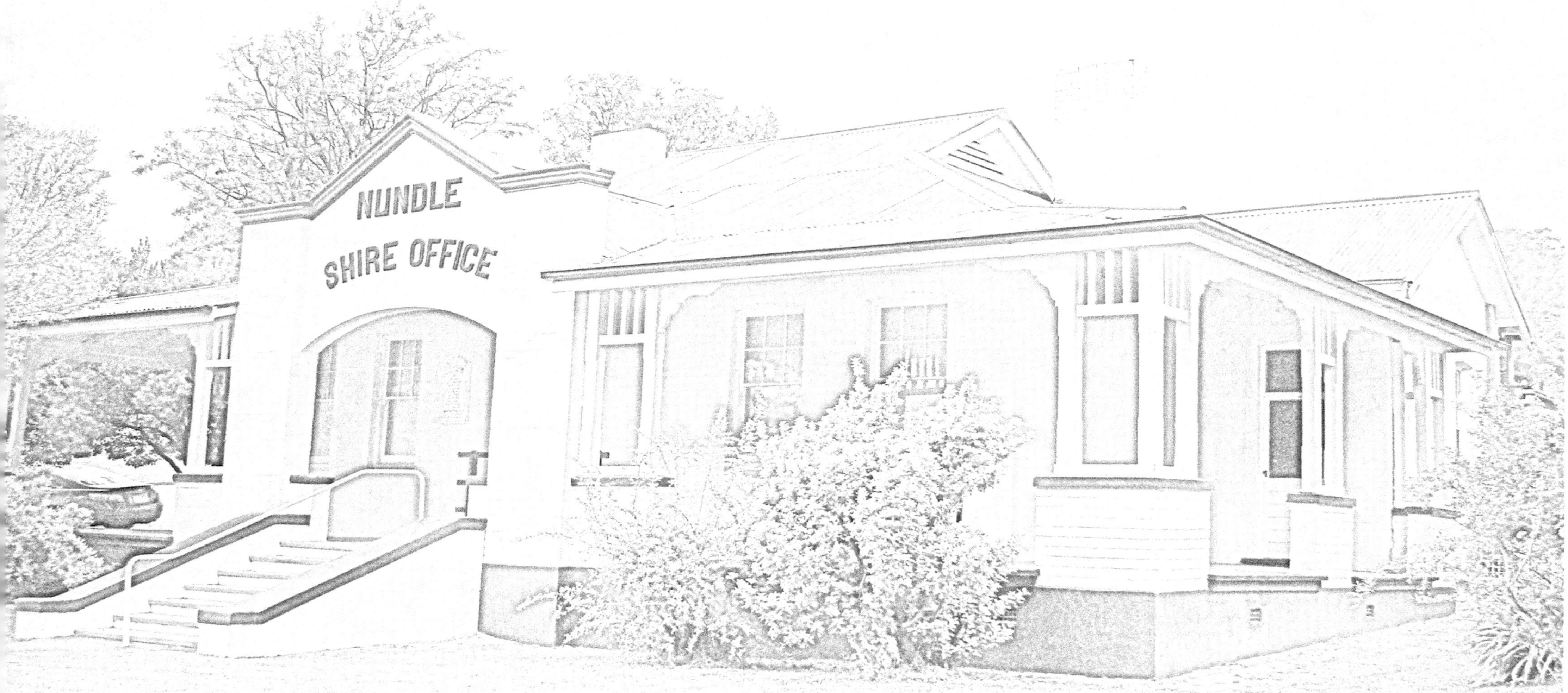
NUNDLE
SHIRE OFFICE

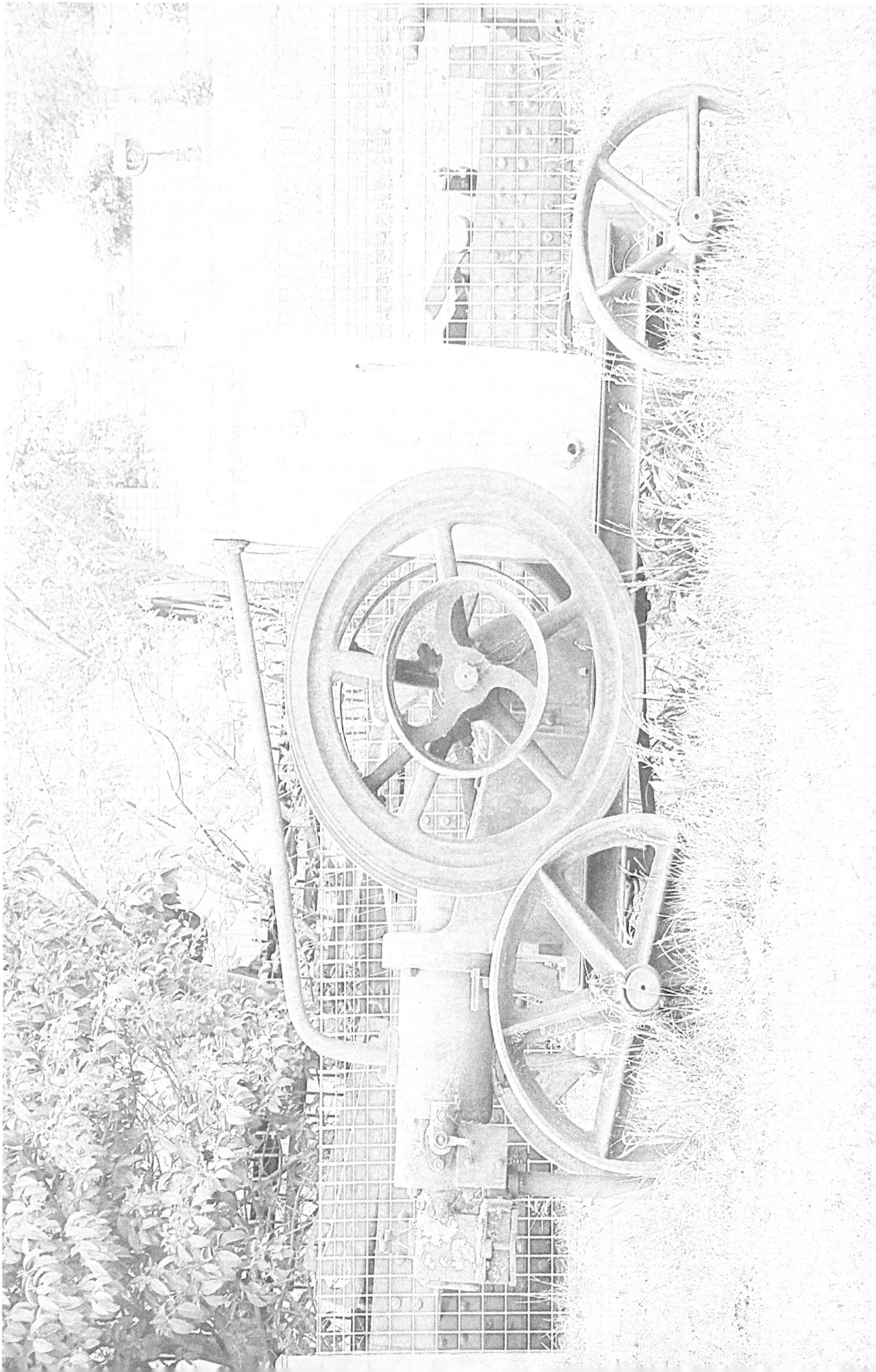

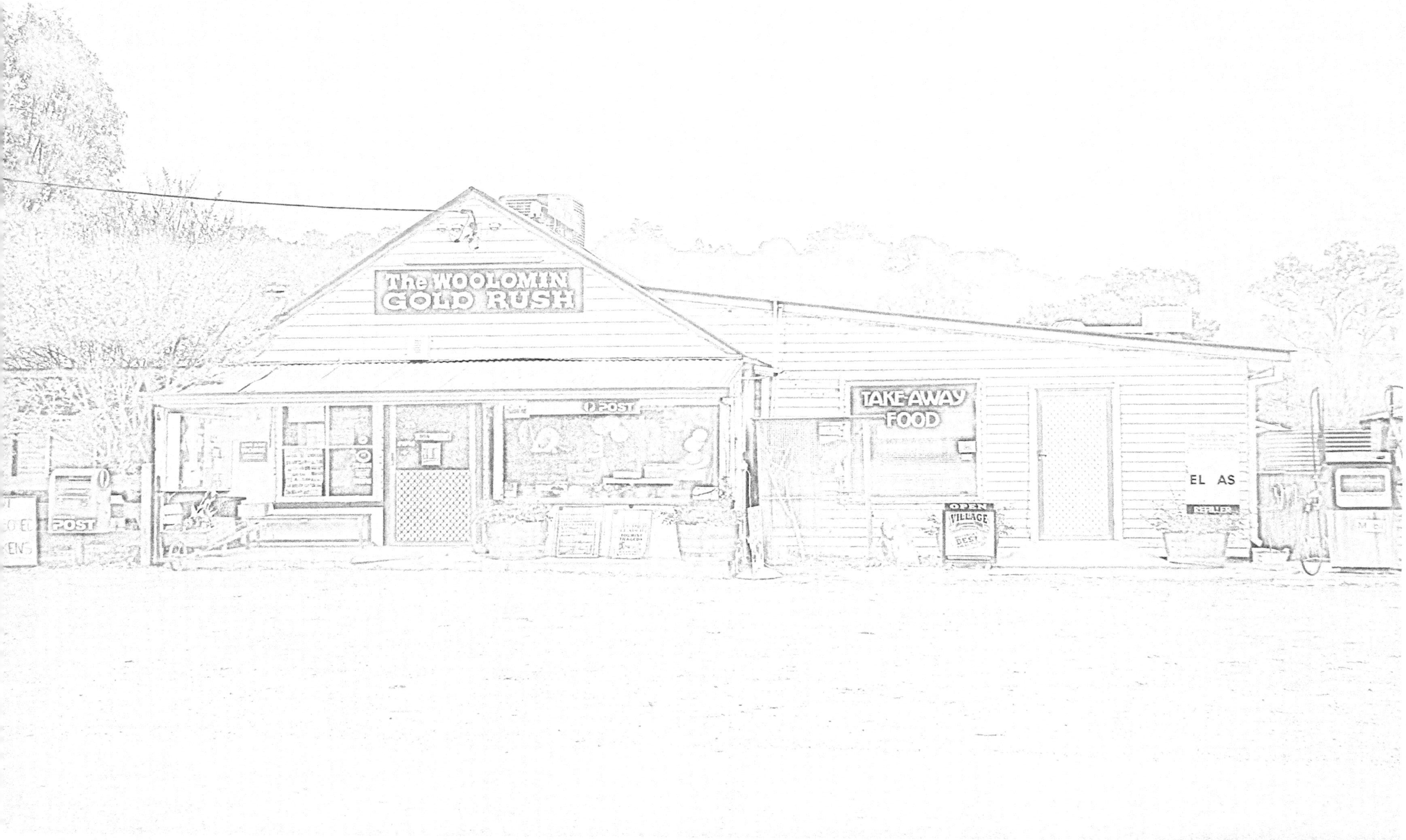
The WOOLOMIN
GOLD RUSH
POST
TAKE-AWAY
FOOD
OPEN
VILLAGE
POST
EL AS

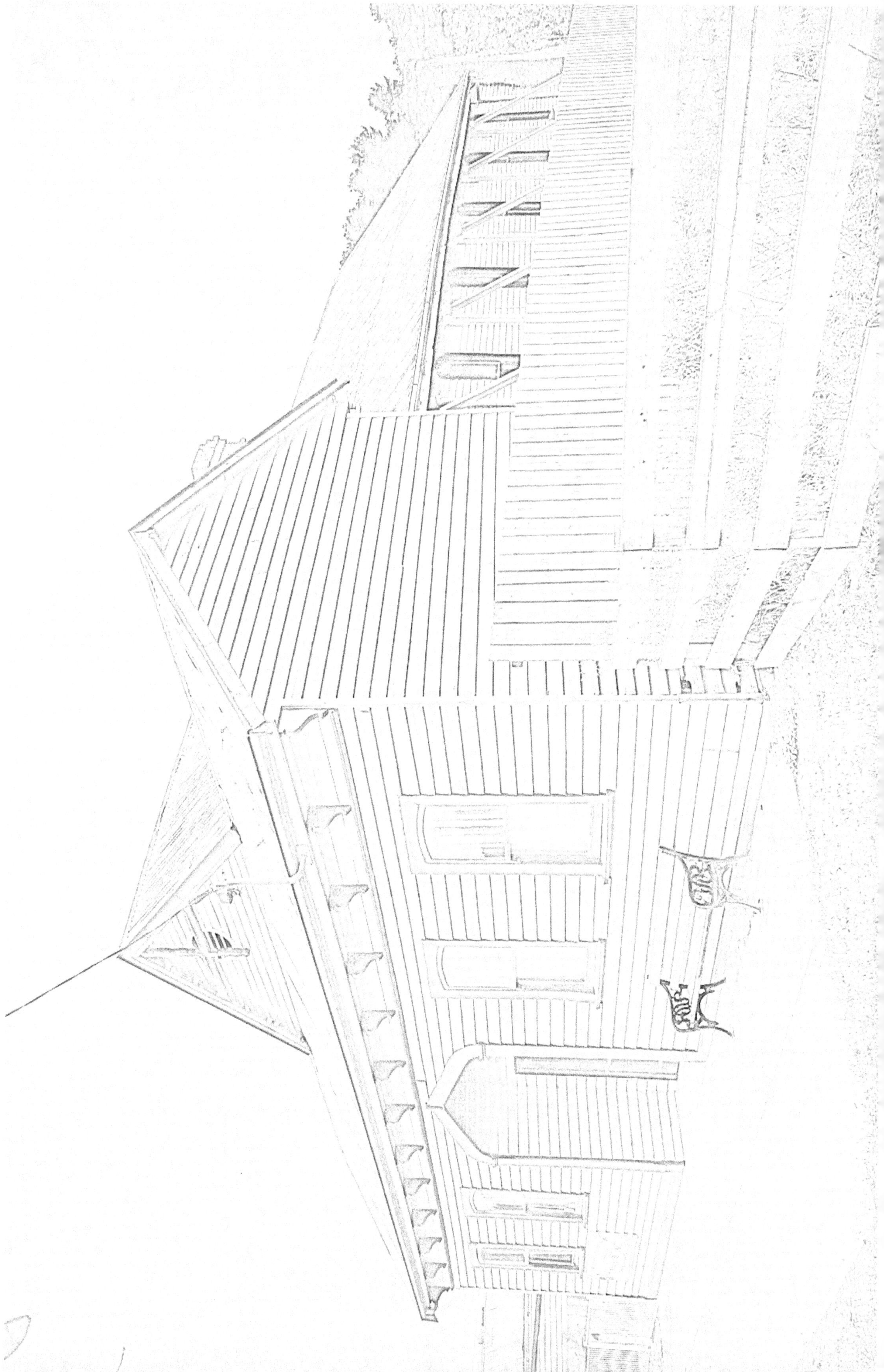

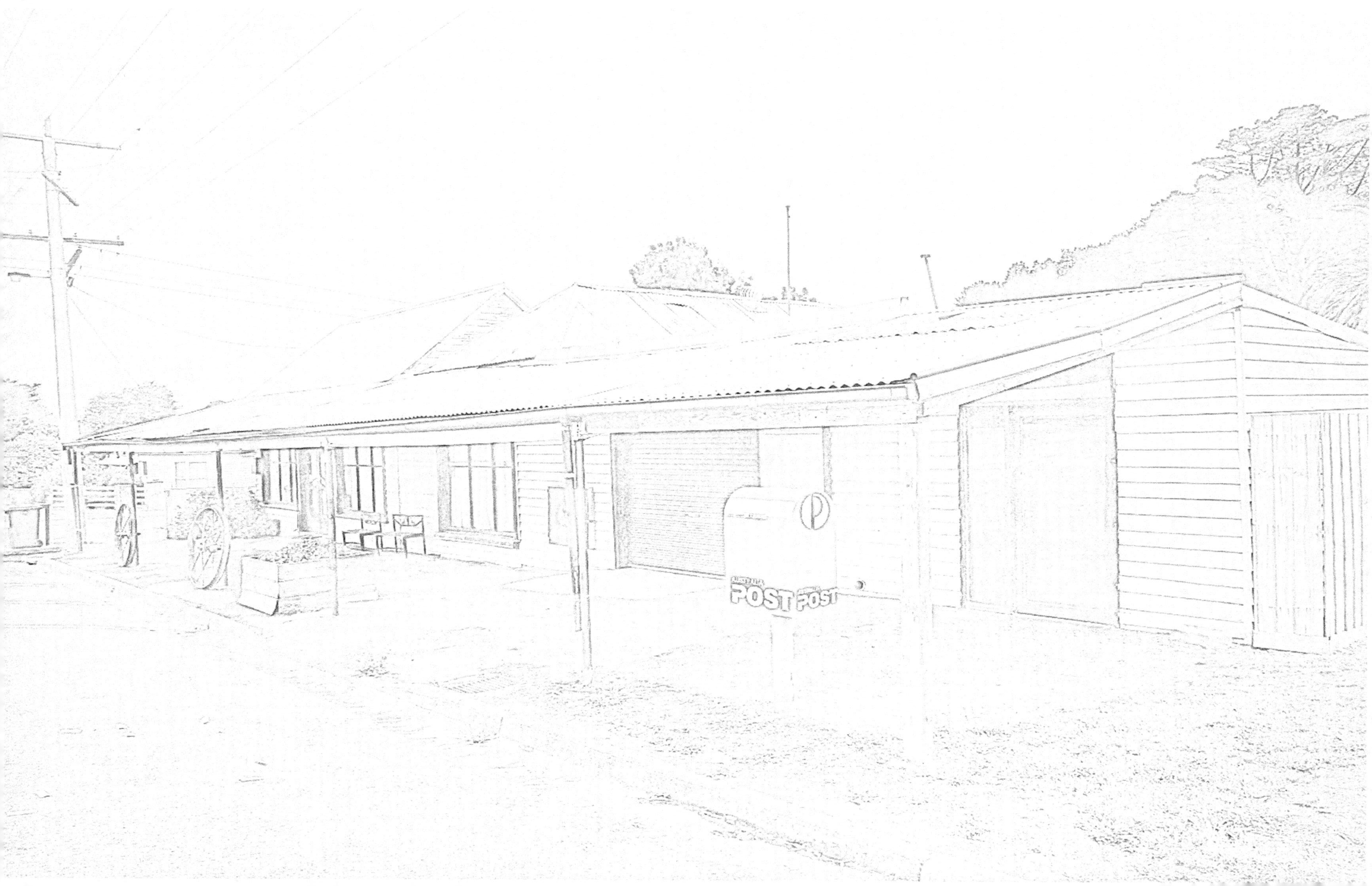
POST
POST

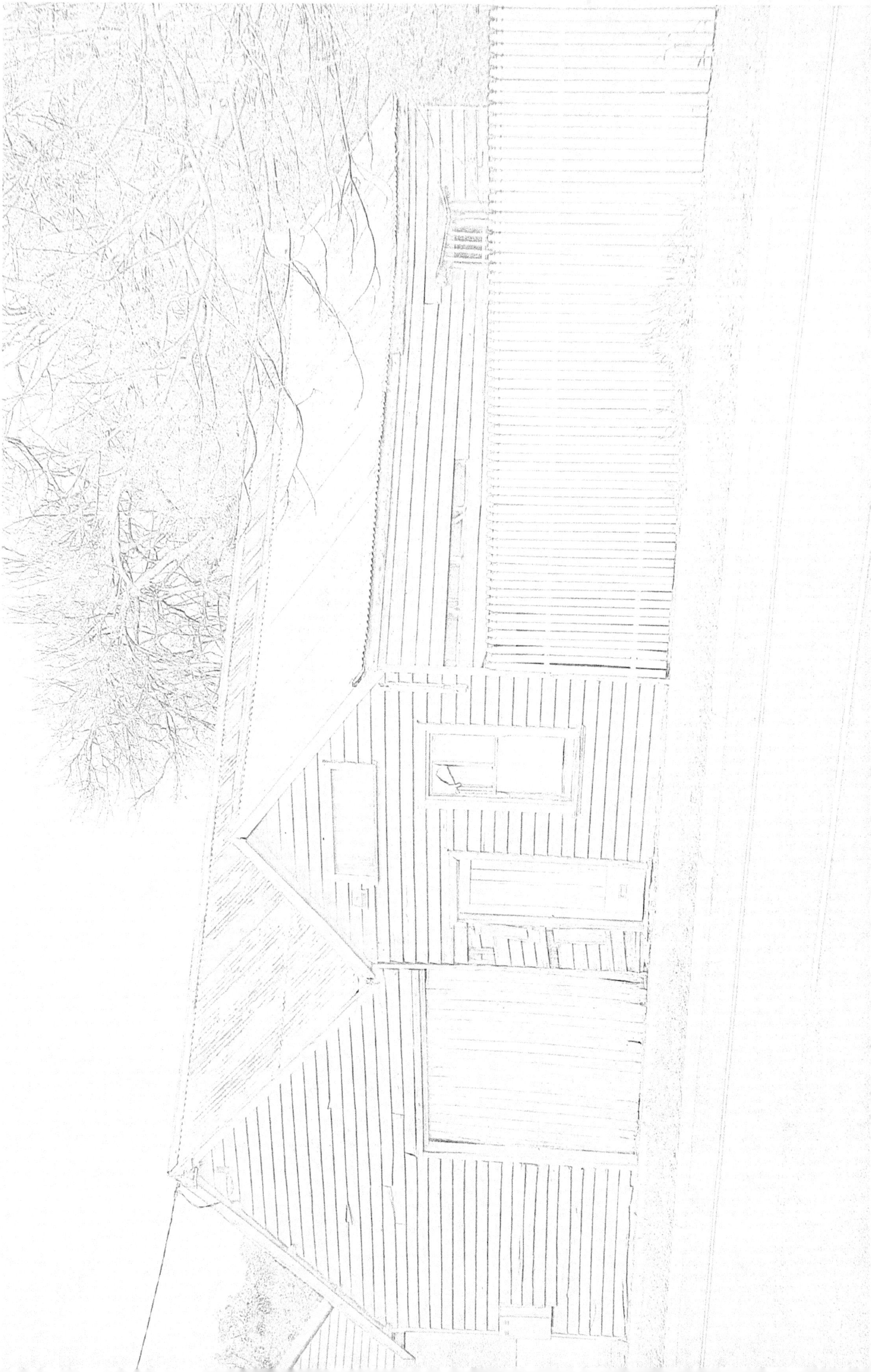

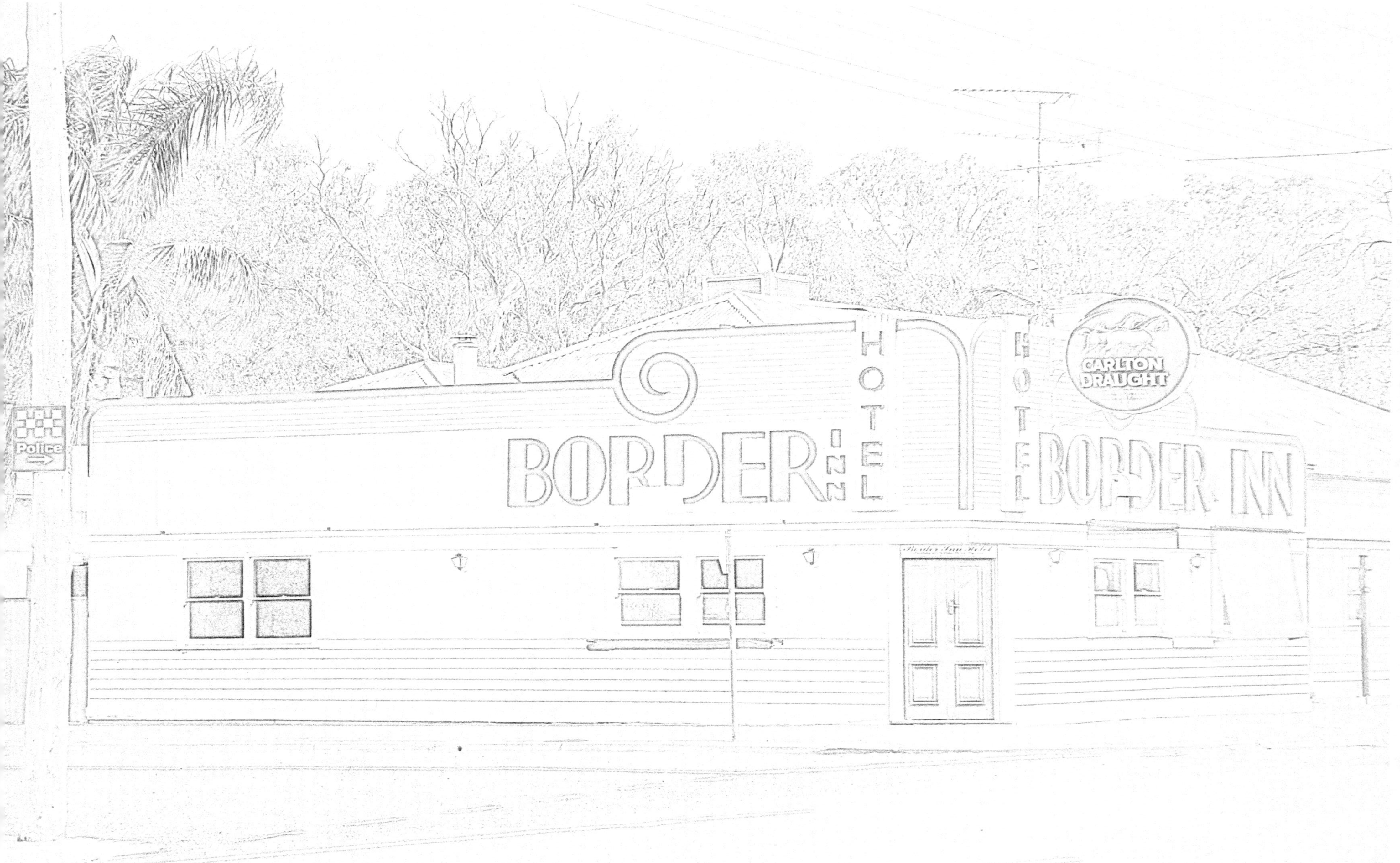
Police
BORDER INN
HOTEL
HOTEL
CARLTON DRAUGHT
BORDER INN

ART-CRAFT CENTRE
ART & CRAFT
MAHOGANY HOUSE

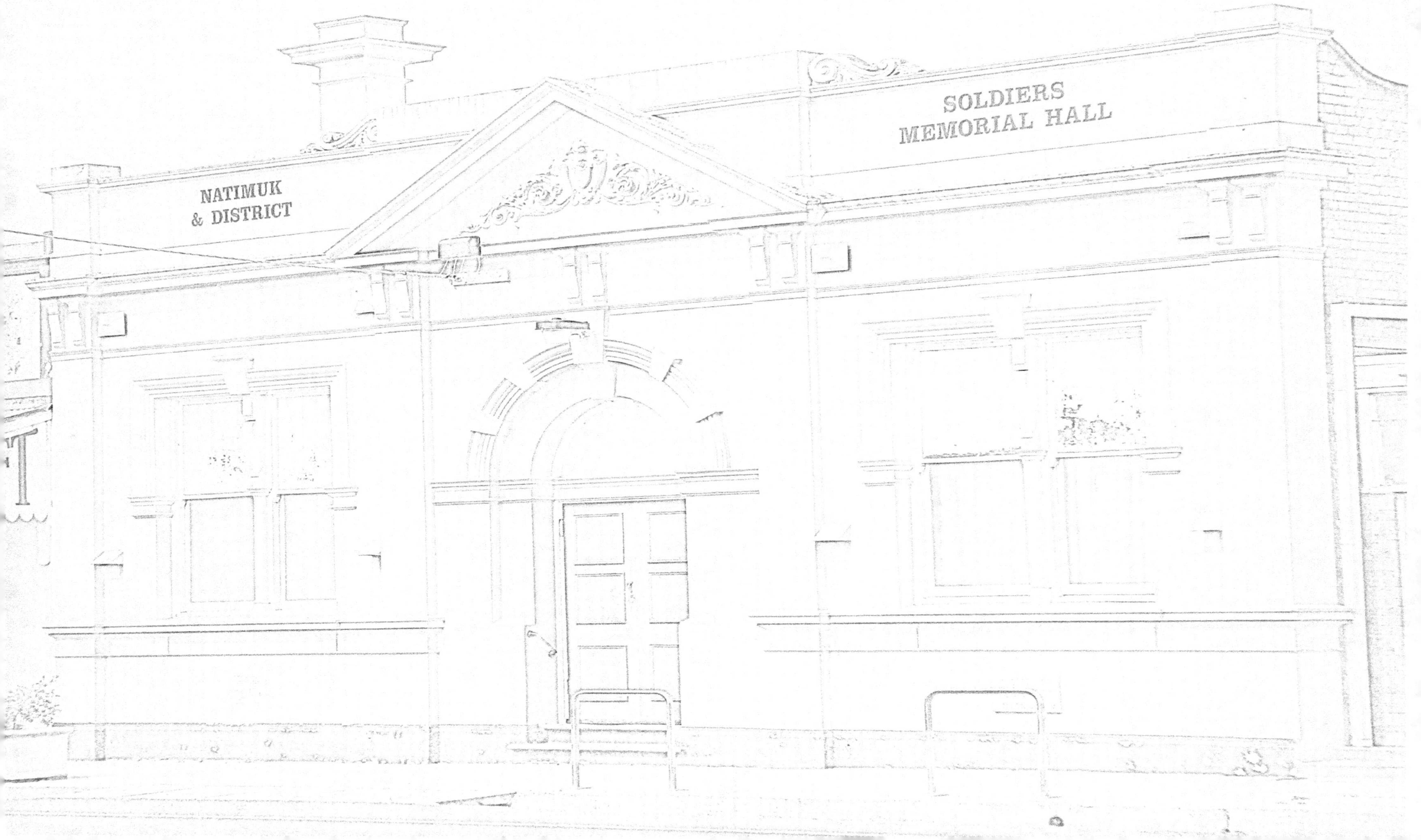
NATIMUK
& DISTRICT
SOLDIERS
MEMORIAL HALL

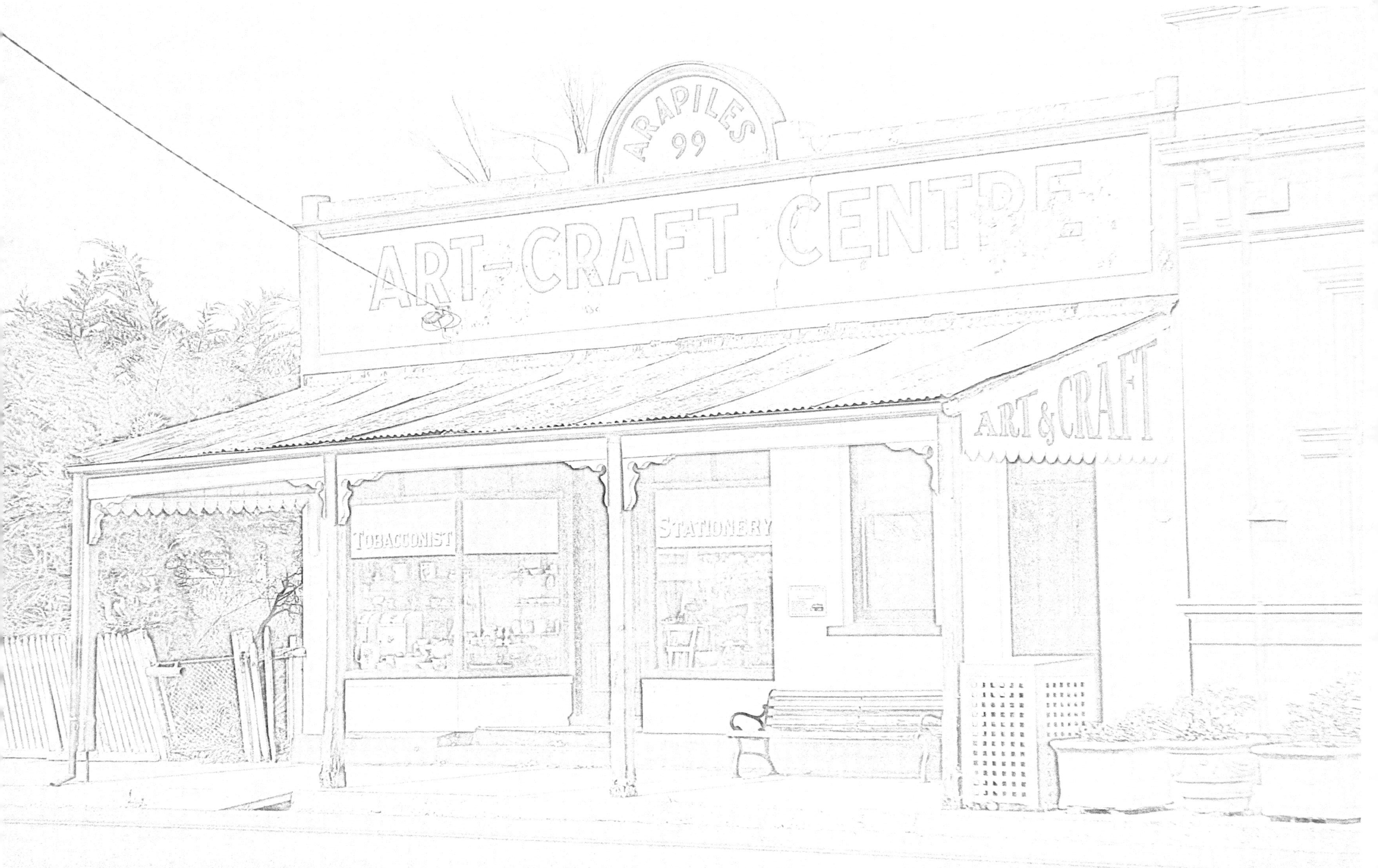
ARAPILES
99
ART-CRAFT CENTRE
ART & CRAFT
TOBACCONIST
STATIONERY

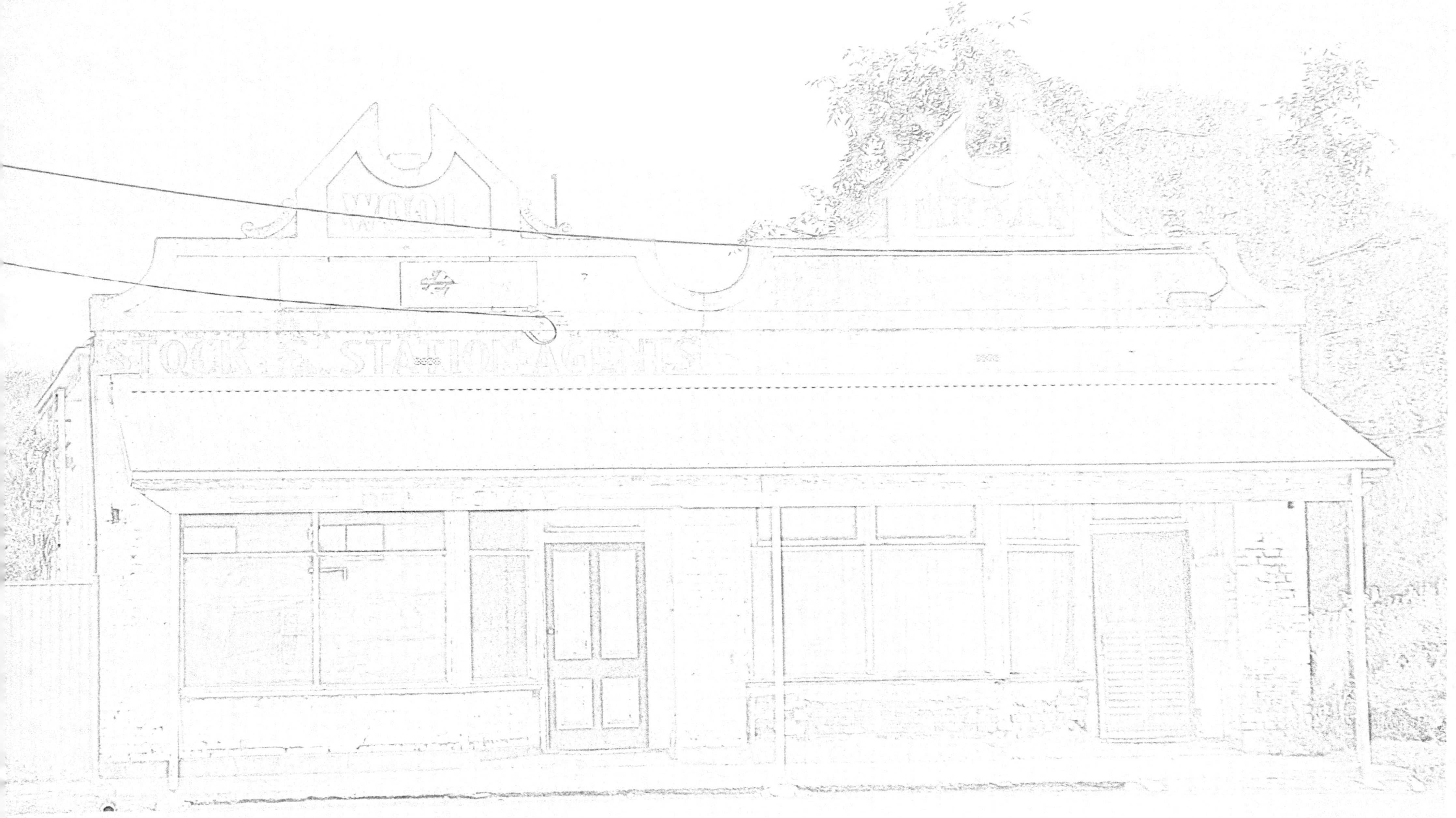
WOOL
STOCK & STATION AGENTS

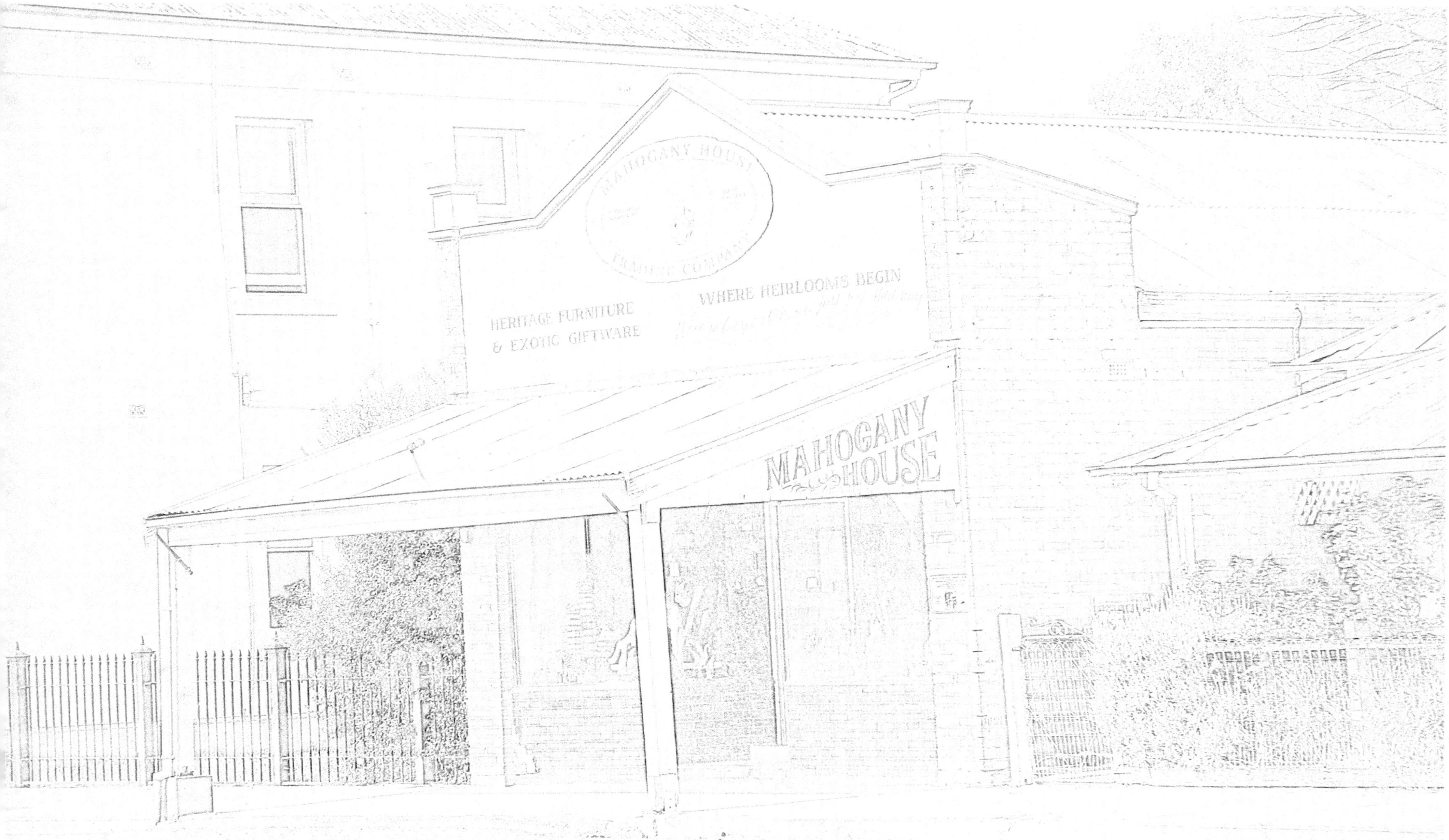
MAHOGANY HOUSE
TRADING COMPANY
HERITAGE FURNITURE
& EXOTIC GIFTWARE
WHERE HEIRLOOMS BEGIN
MAHOGANY HOUSE

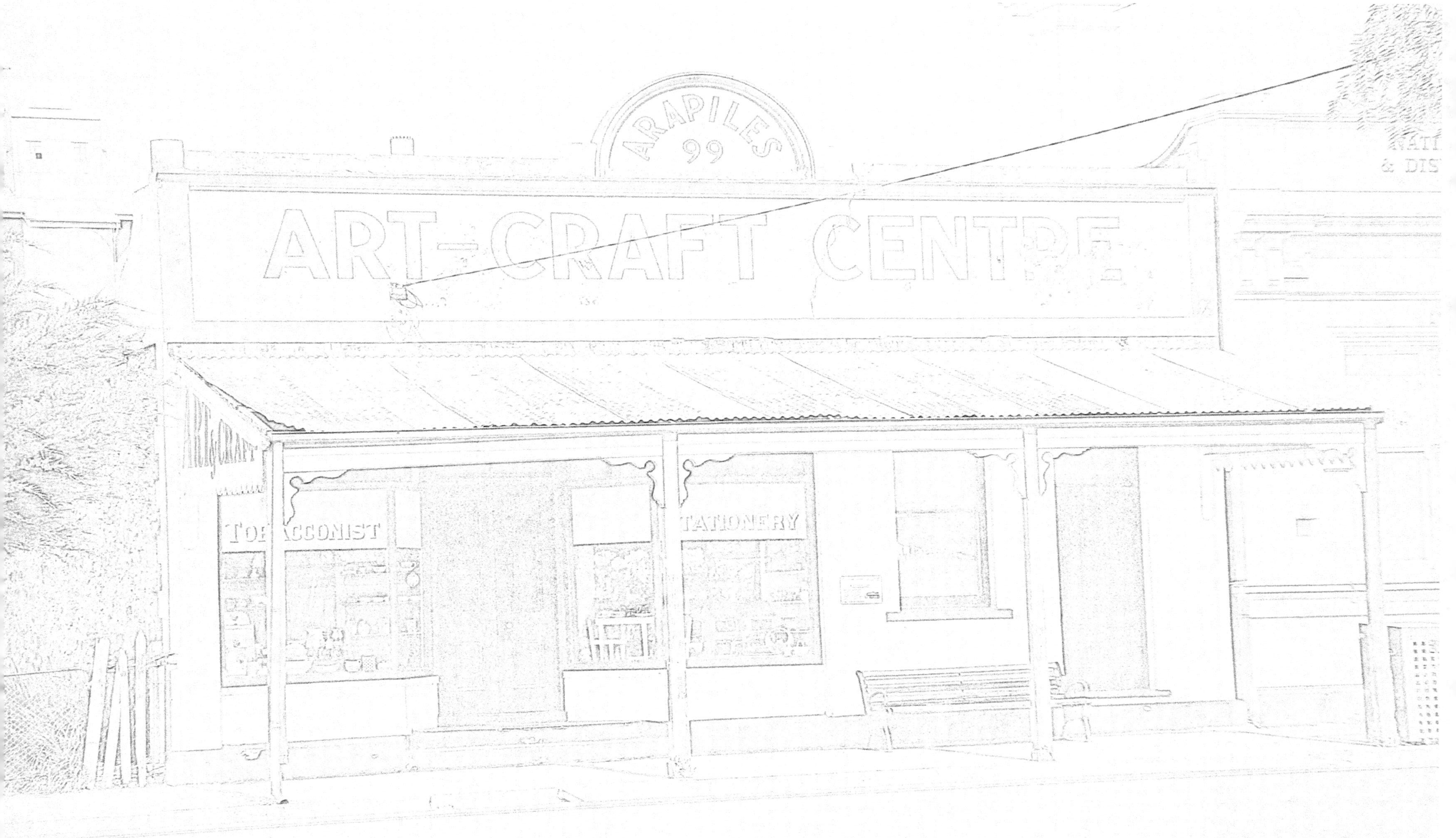
ARAPILES
99
ART-CRAFT CENTRE
STATIONERY
ACCONIST

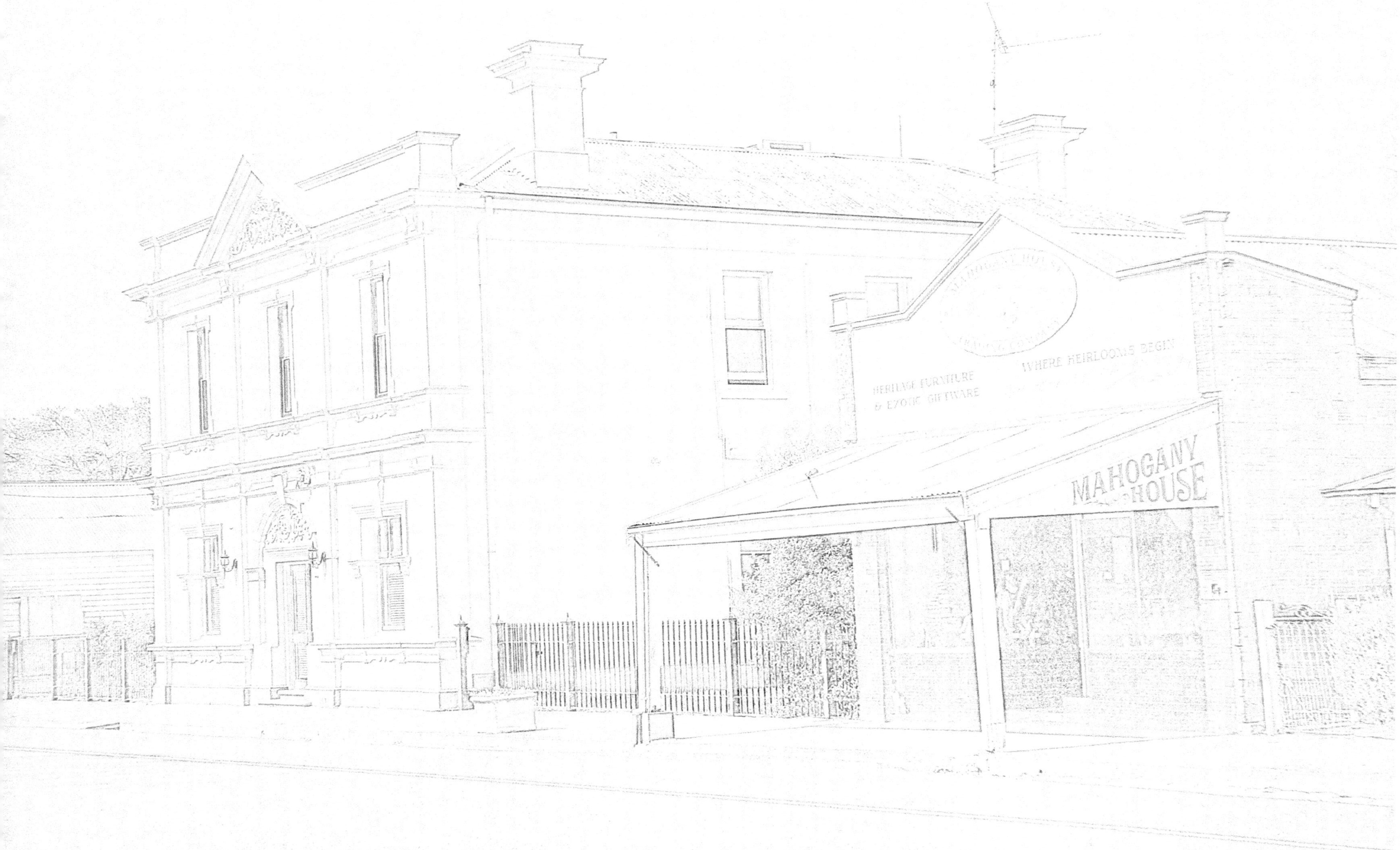
WHERE HEIRLOOMS BEGIN
HERITAGE FURNITURE
& EXOTIC GIFTWARE
MAHOGANY
HOUSE

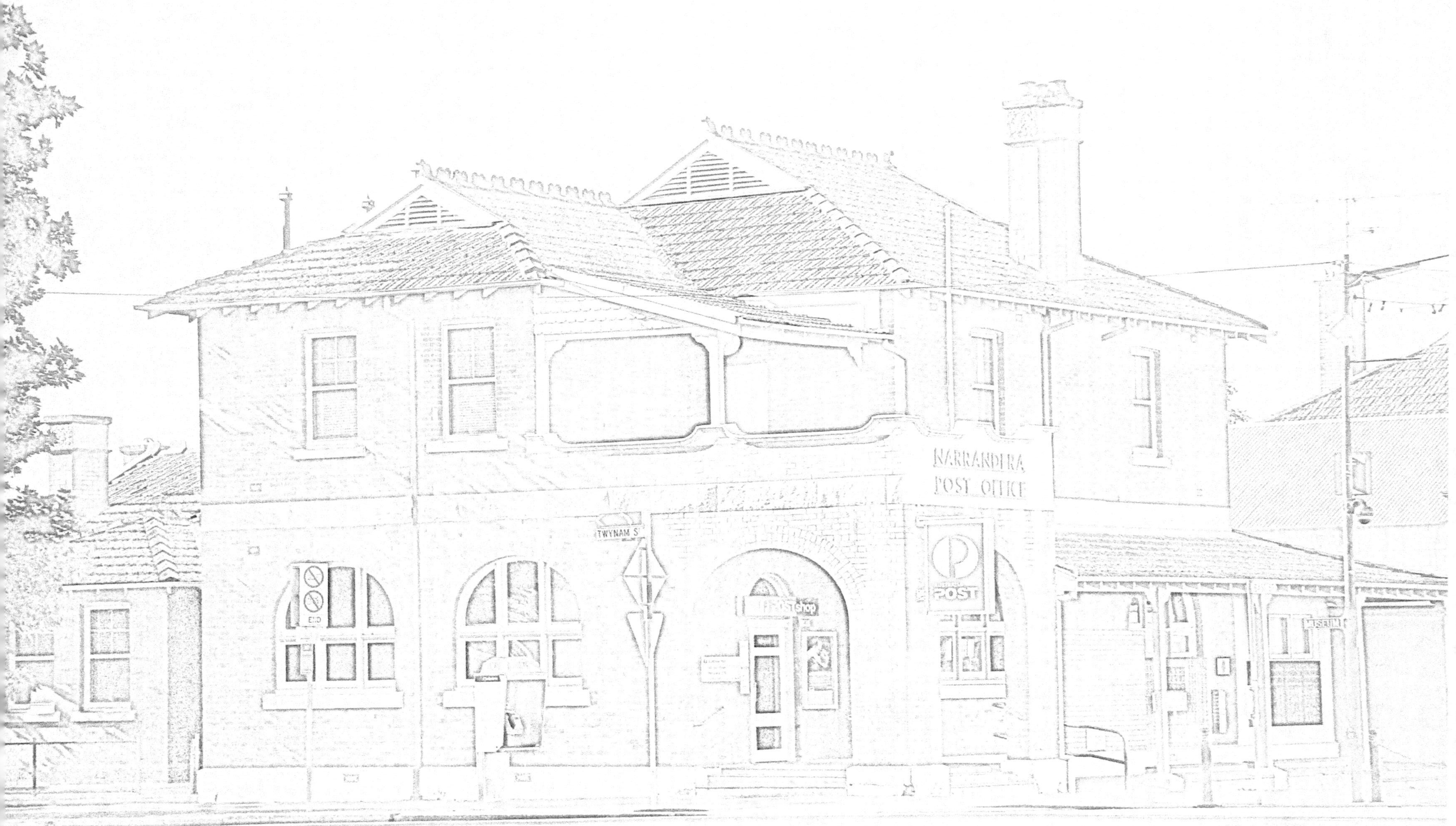
NARRANDERA
POST OFFICE
POST
POST Shop
TWYNAM ST
END
MUSEUM

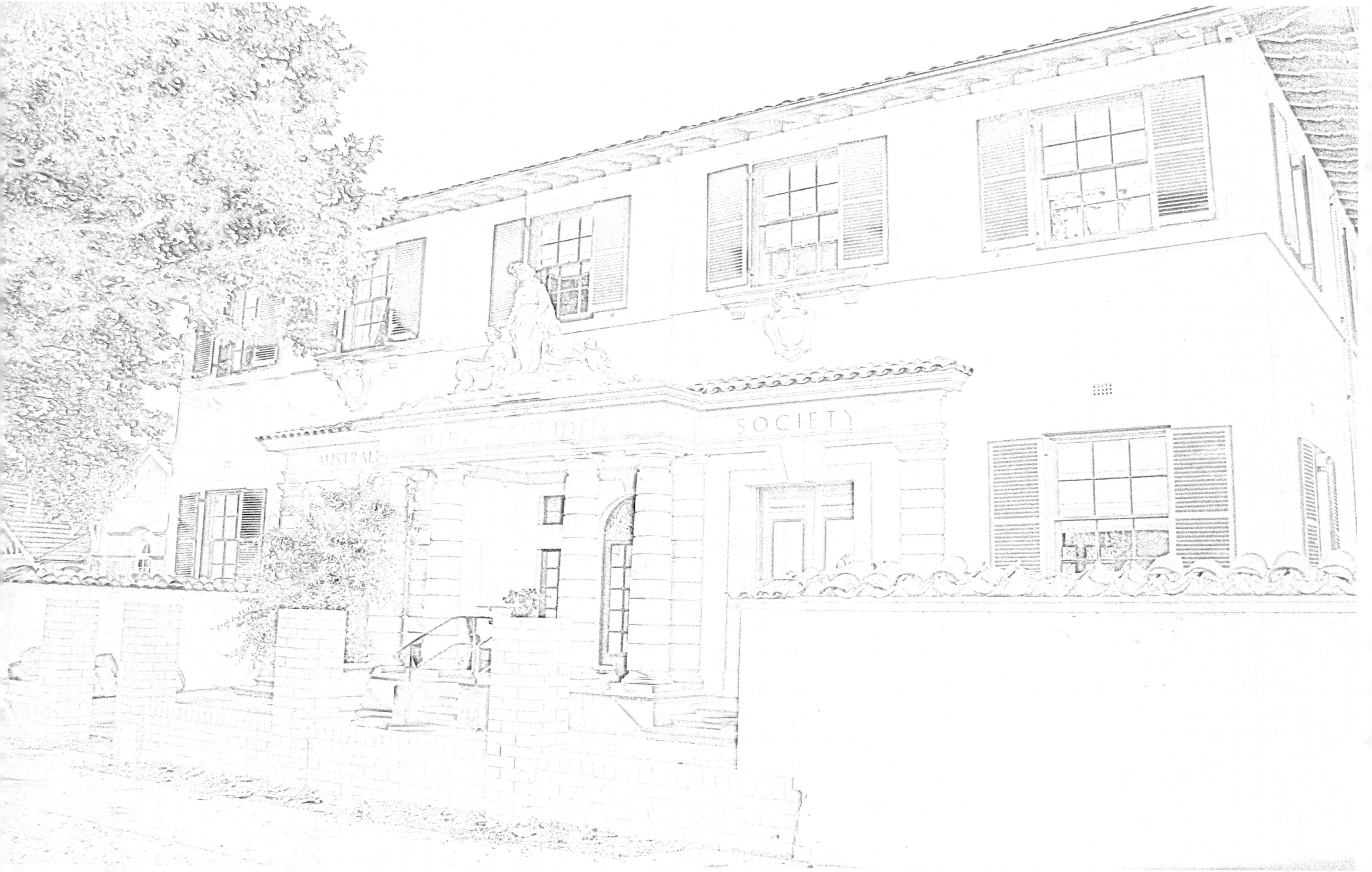
SOCIETY

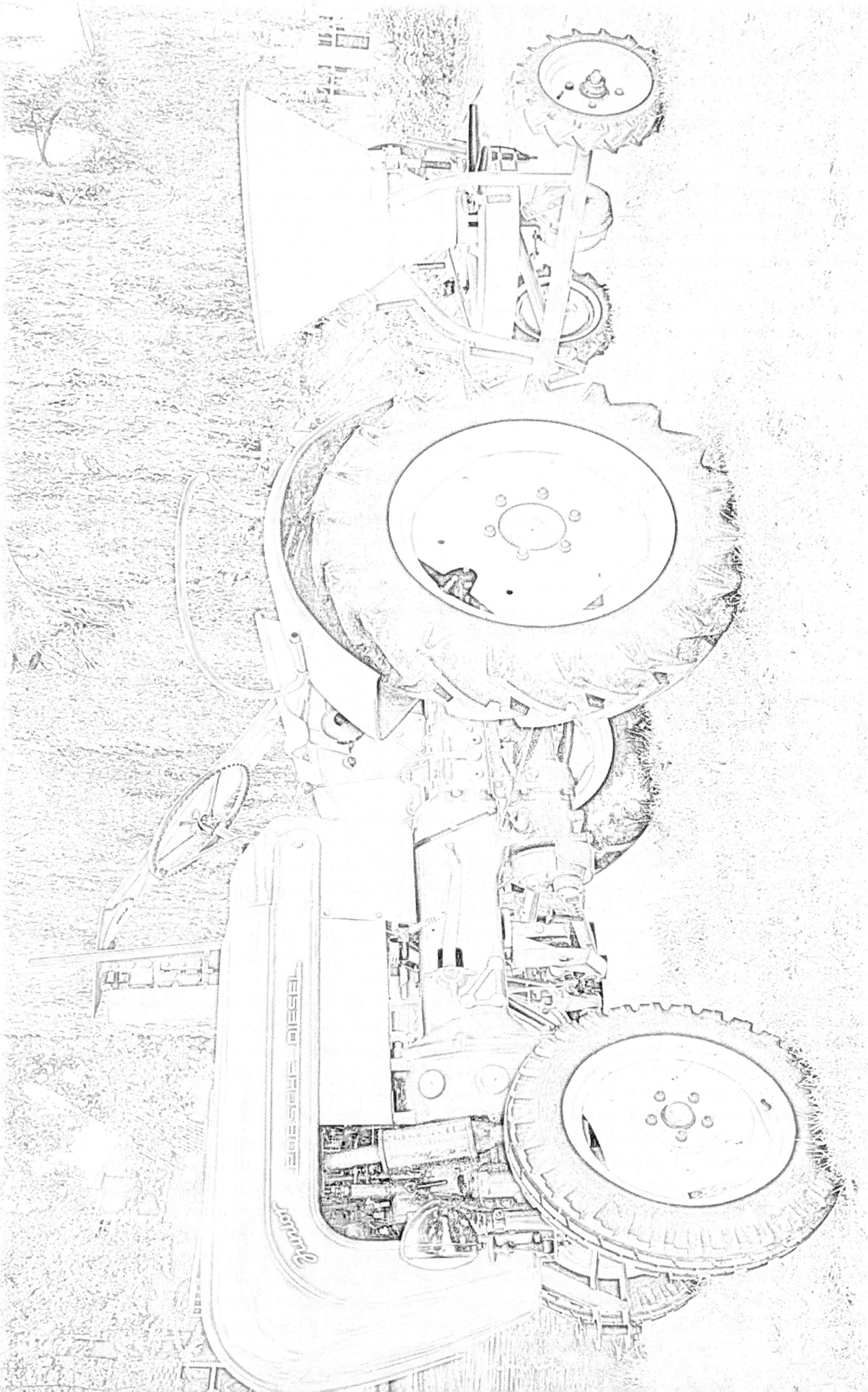
PORSCHE DIESEL

NOW OPEN
THE PANCAKE KITCHEN
LOVELY!
OPEN 7 DAYS
7:30AM - 10:00PM

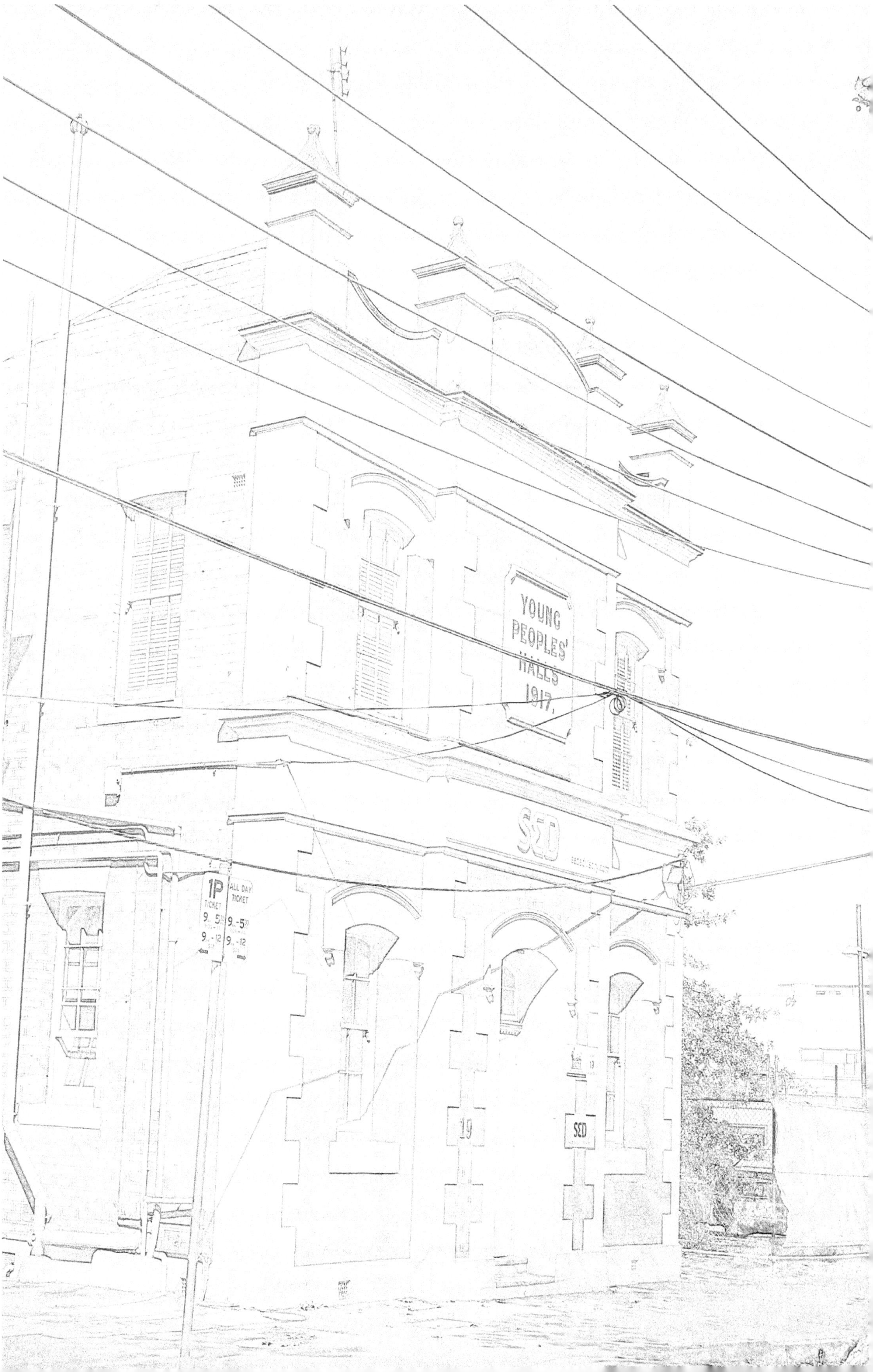
YOUNG
PEOPLES'
HALLS
1917.
SED
1P
TICKET
ALL DAY
TICKET
19
SED

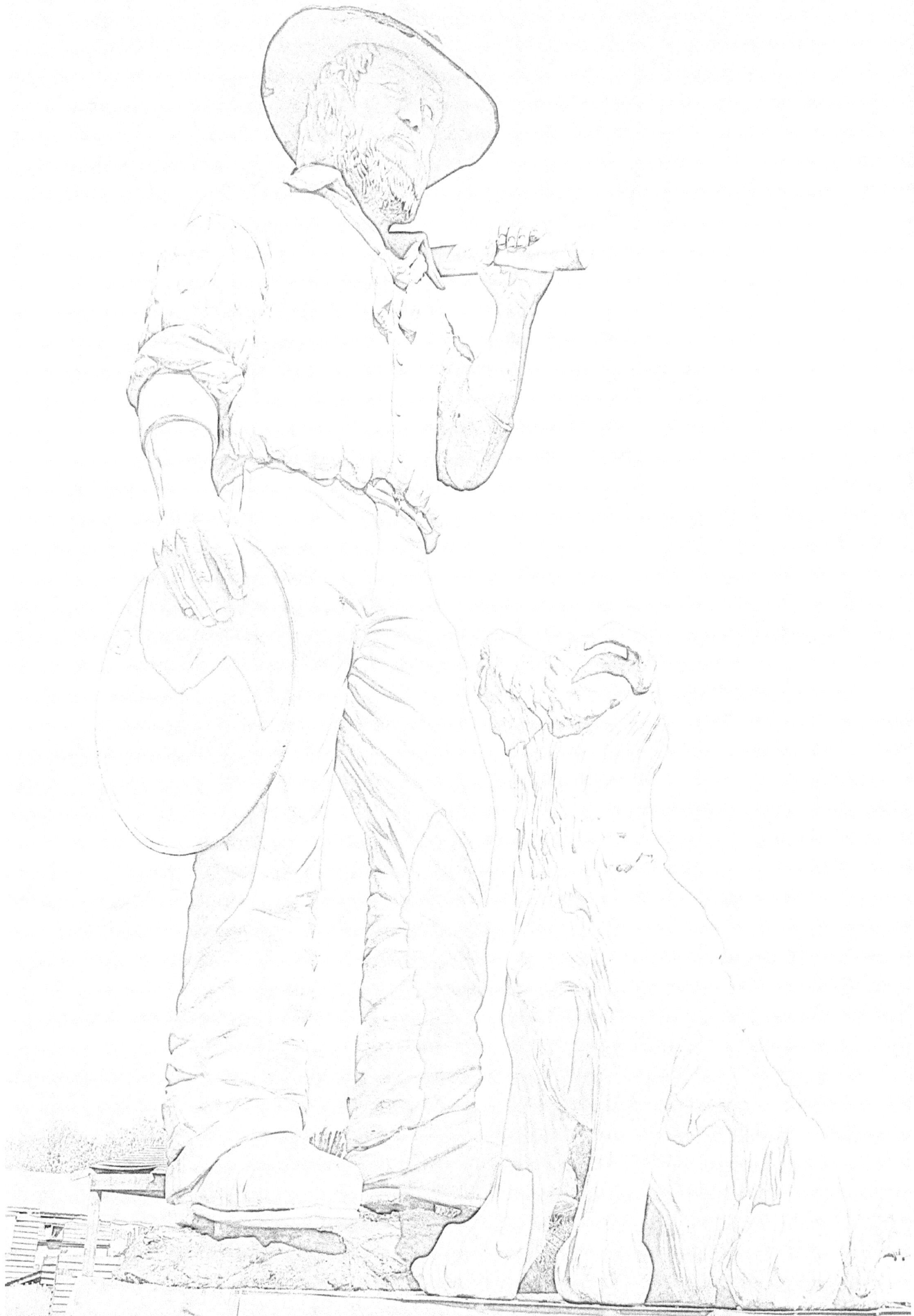

1856
BALLARAT
FIRE STATION

Forrest Op Shop
DIOCESE of BALLARAT
ANGLICAN
PARISH OF THE OTWAYS
St. JAMES CHURCH
PARISH PRIEST

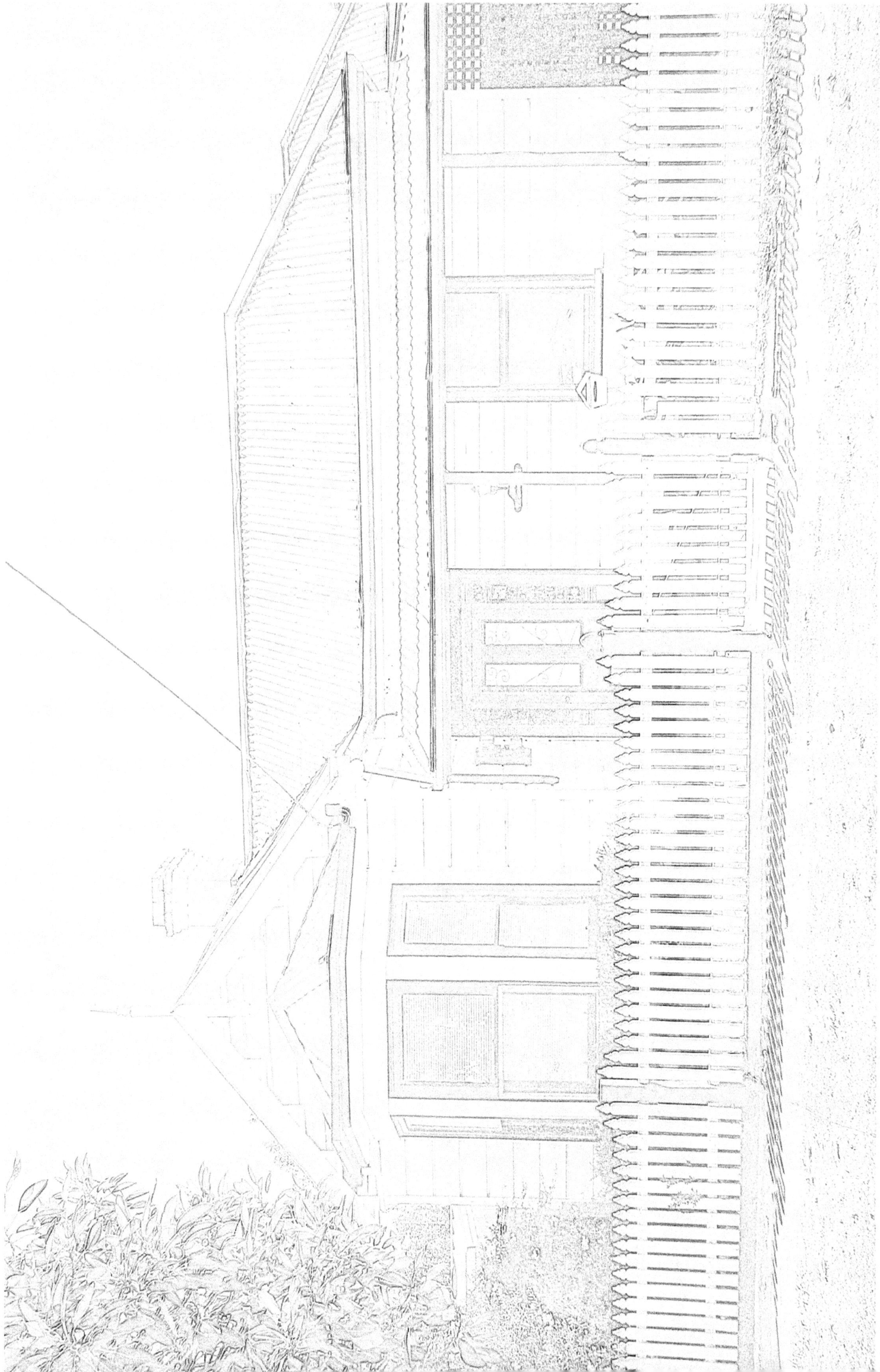

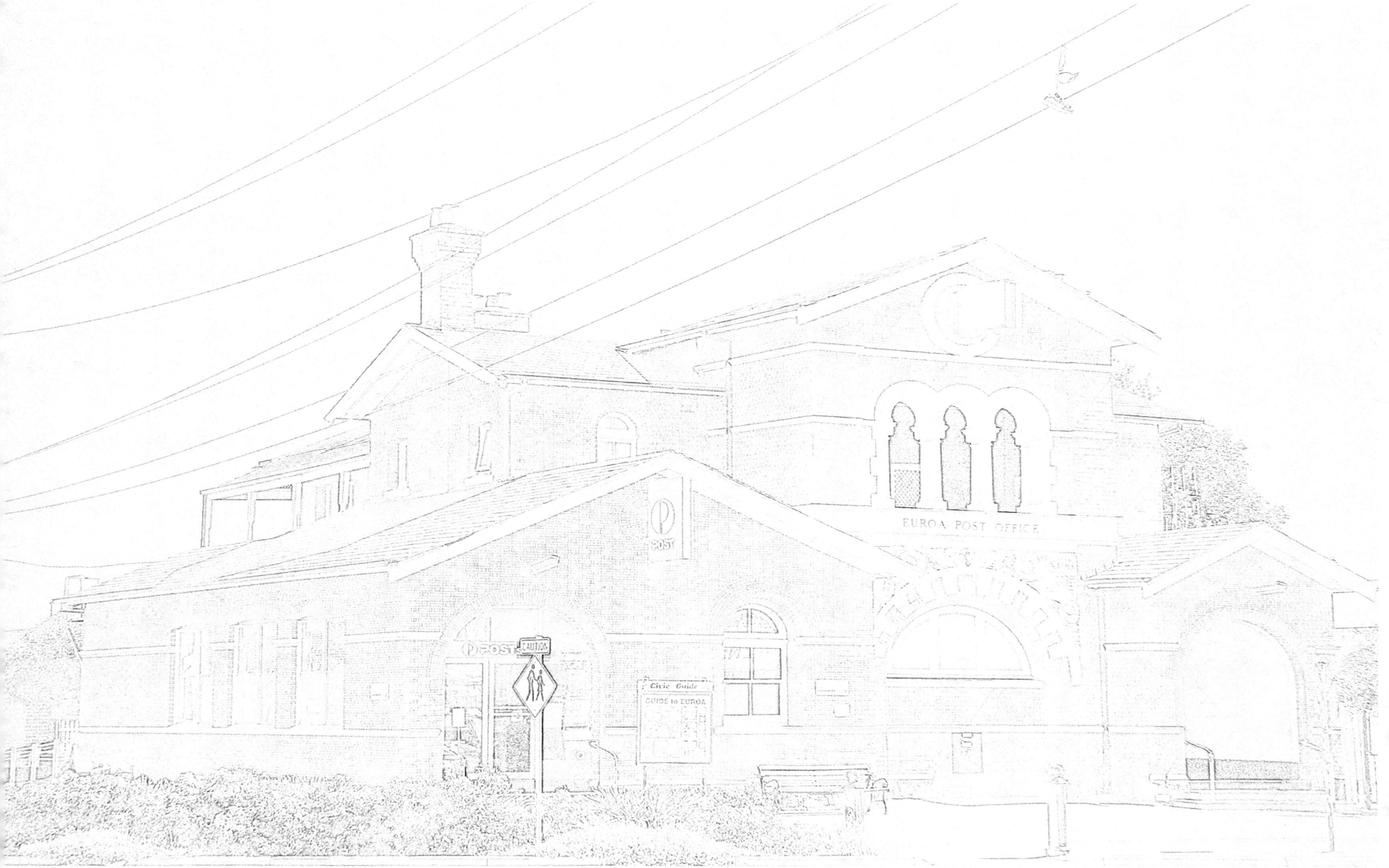
EUROA POST OFFICE
POST
POST
CAUTION
Civic Guide
GUIDE to EUROA

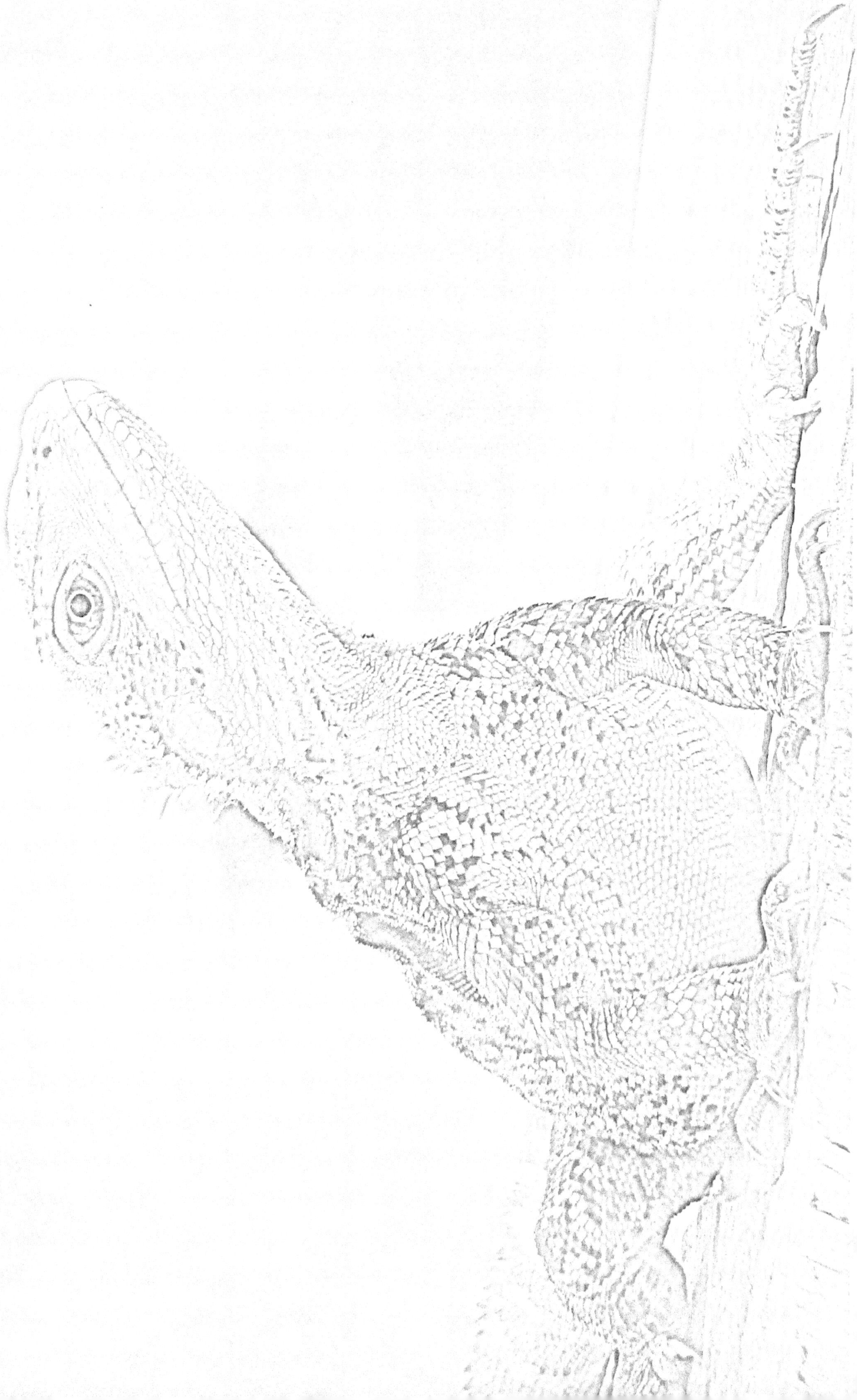

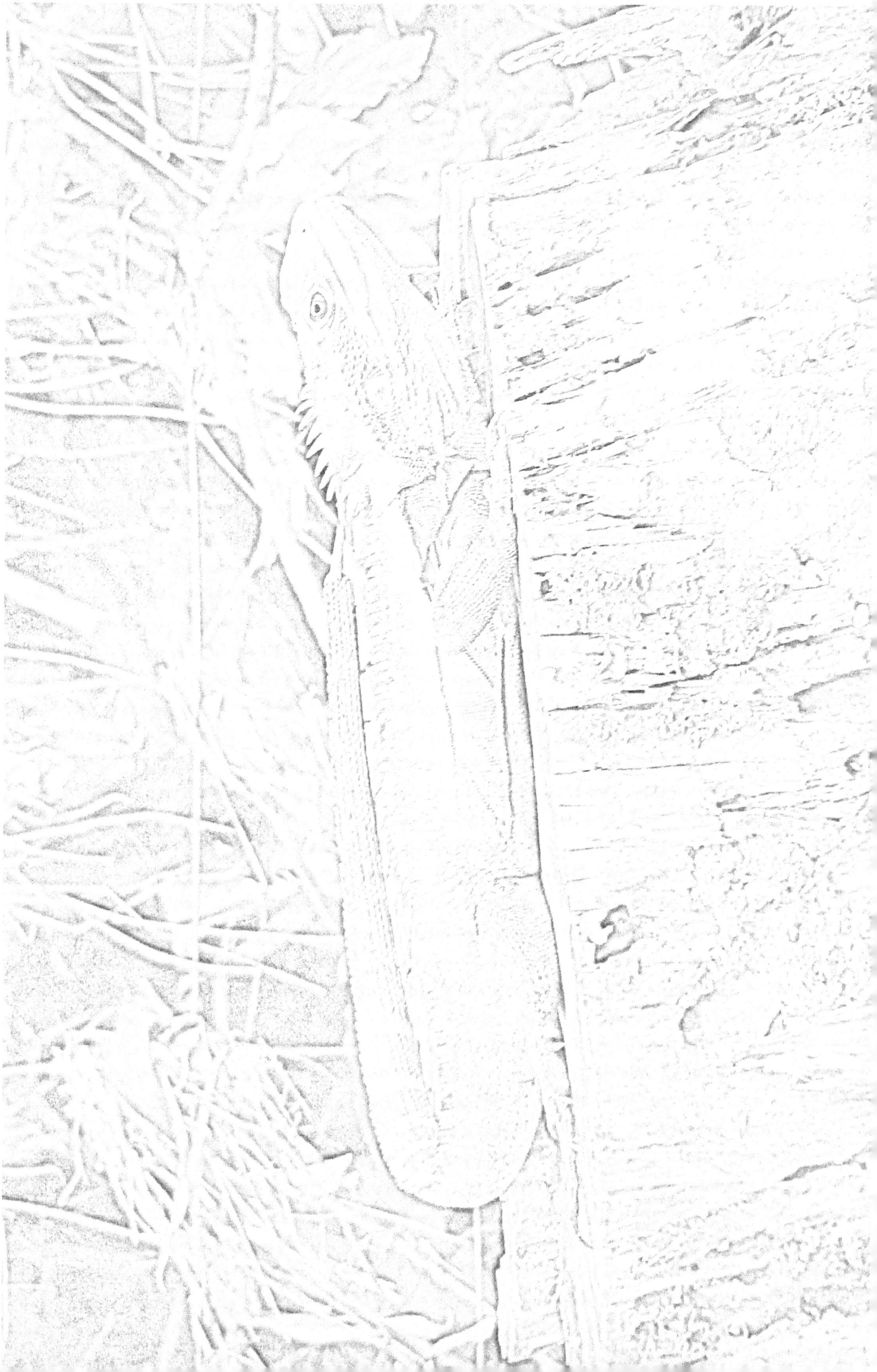

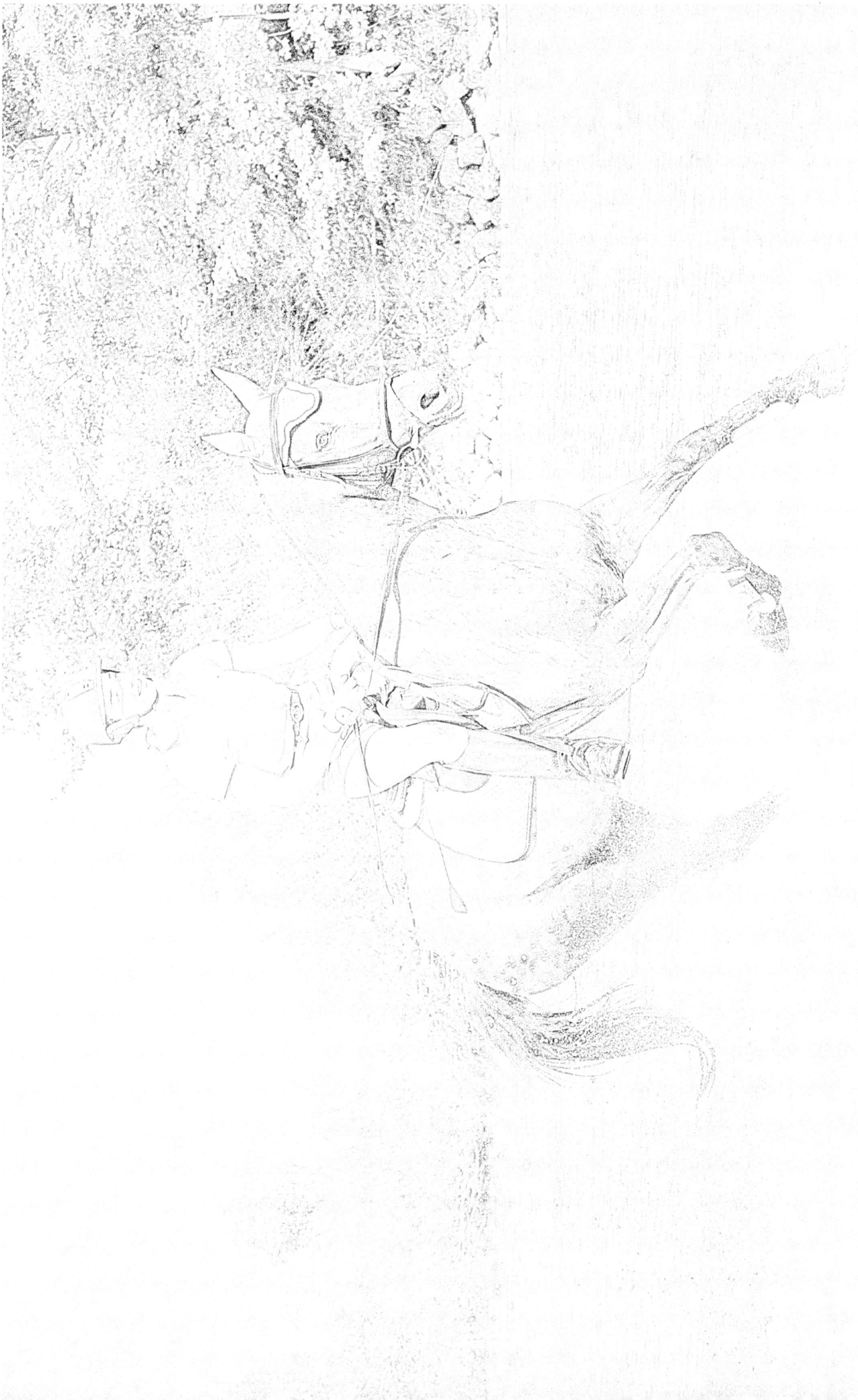

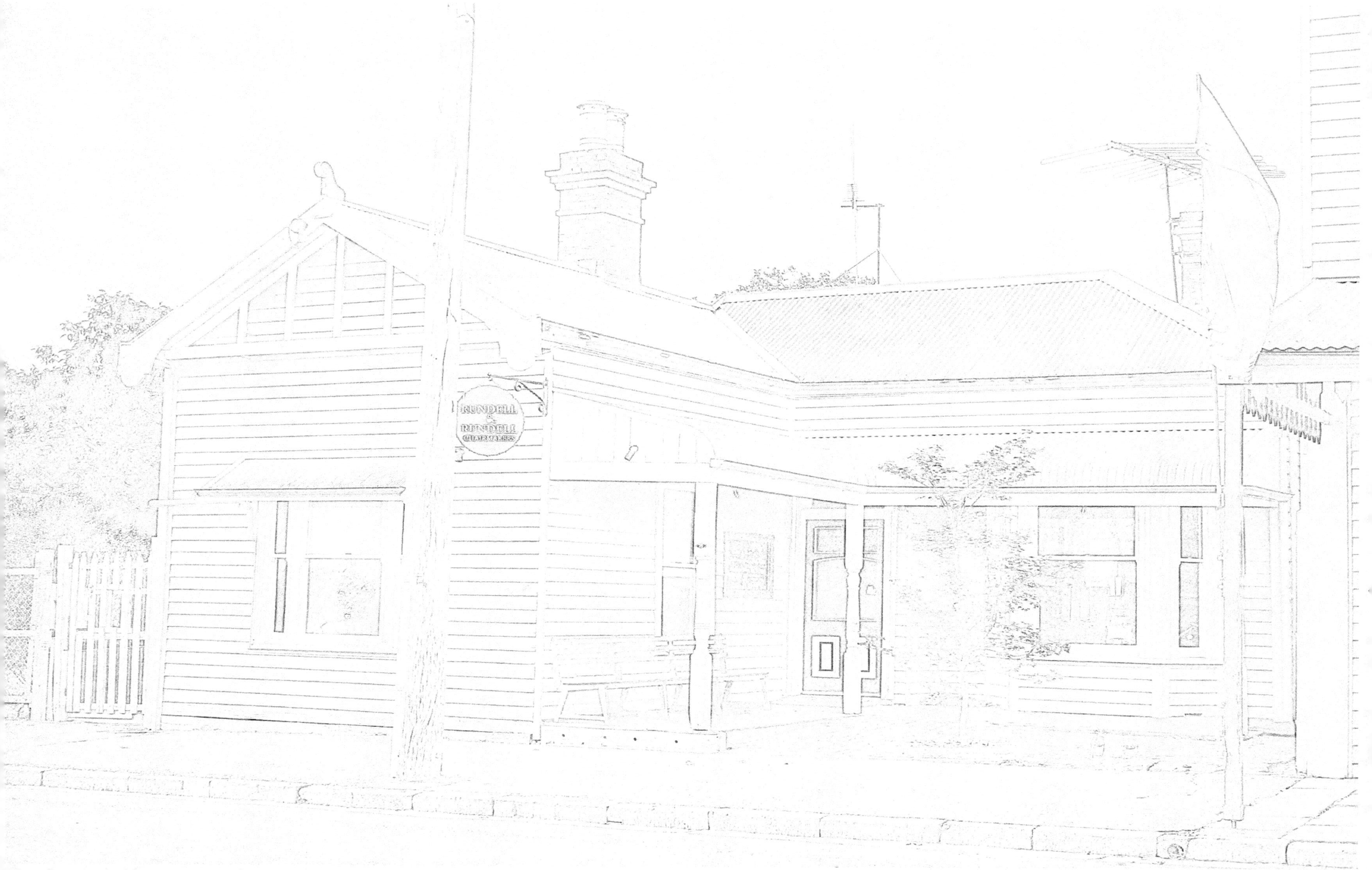
RUNDELL
&
RUNDELL

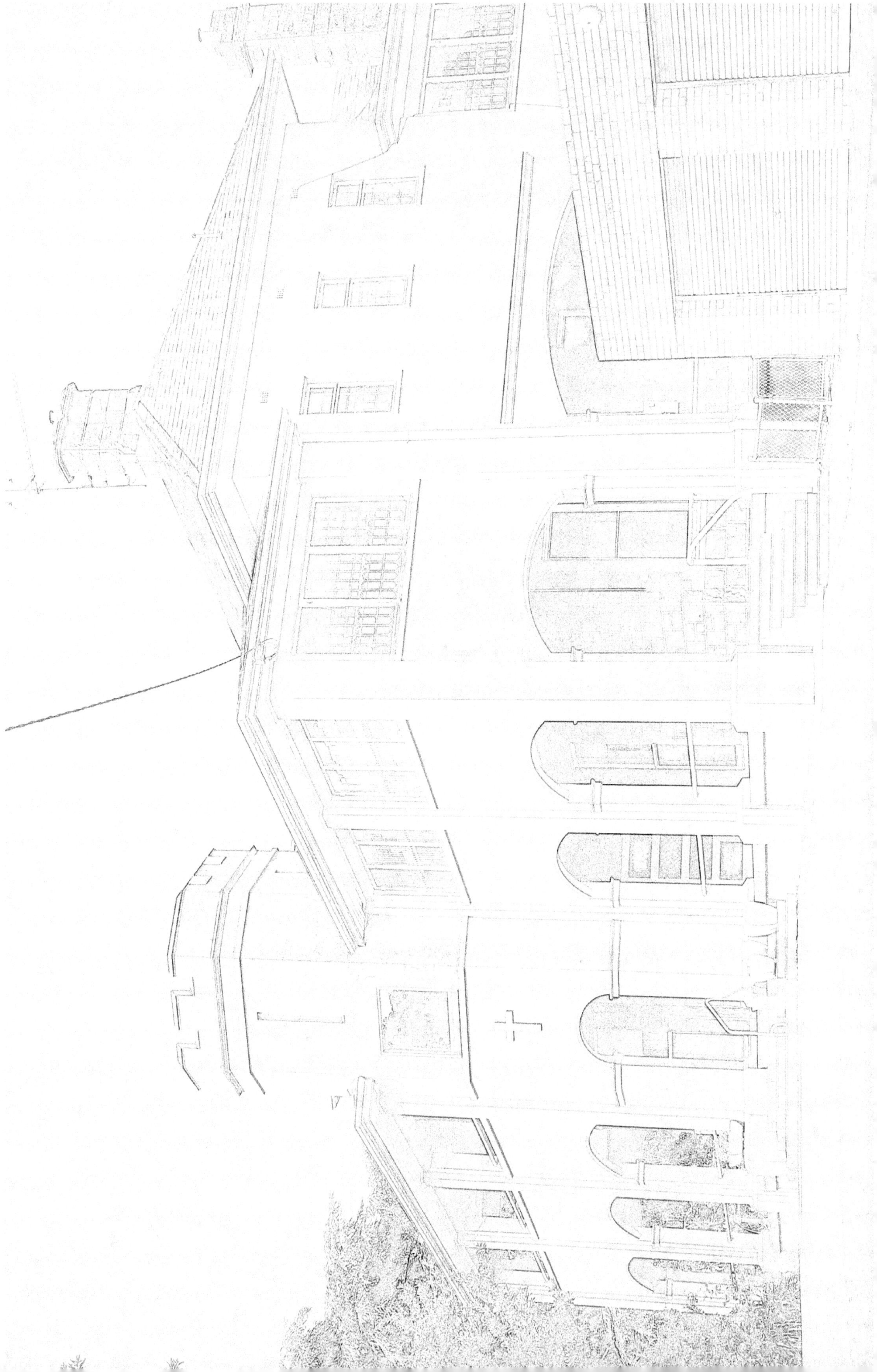

DRIVE

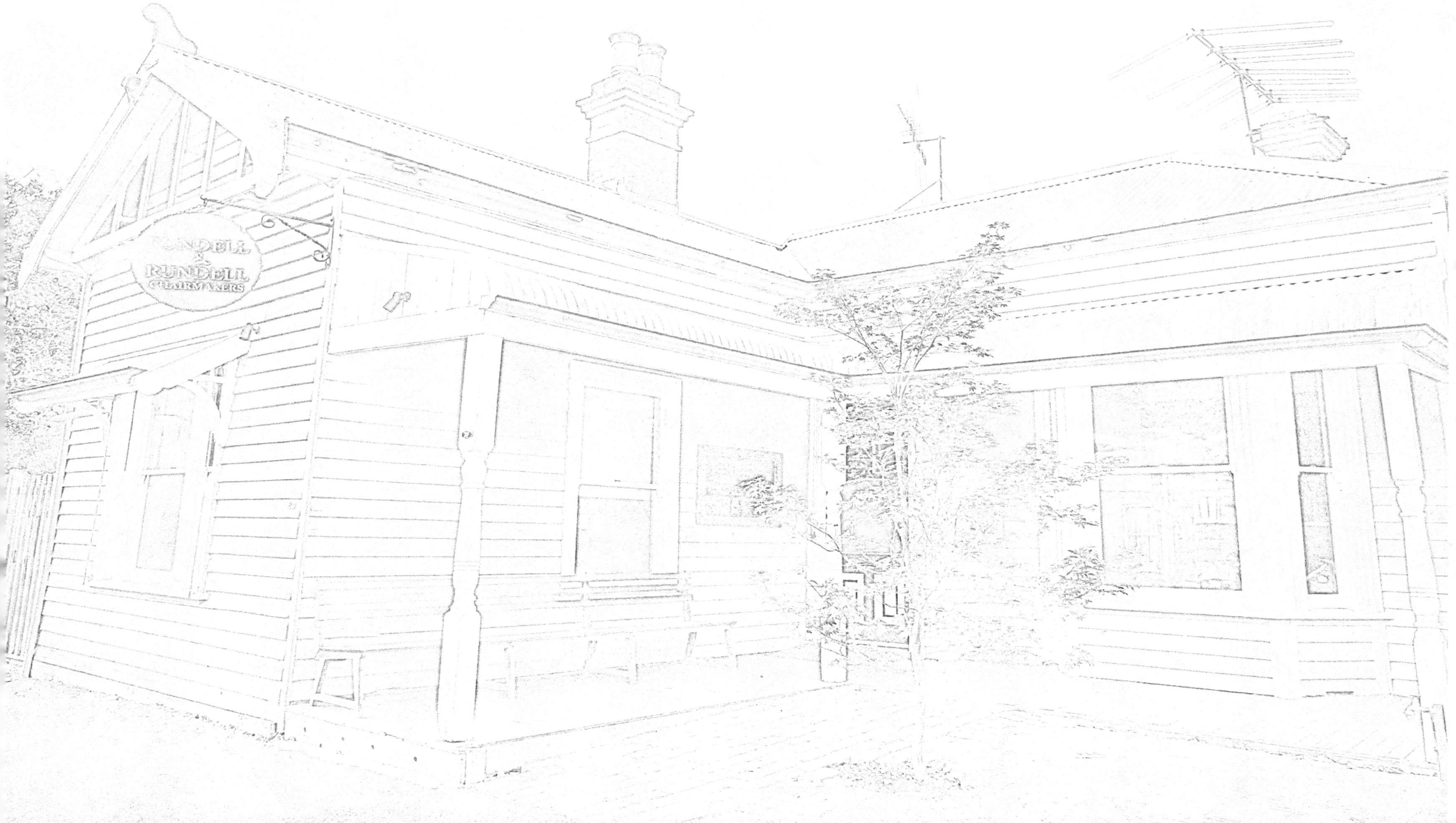
RUNDELL
&
RUNDELL
CHAIRMAKERS

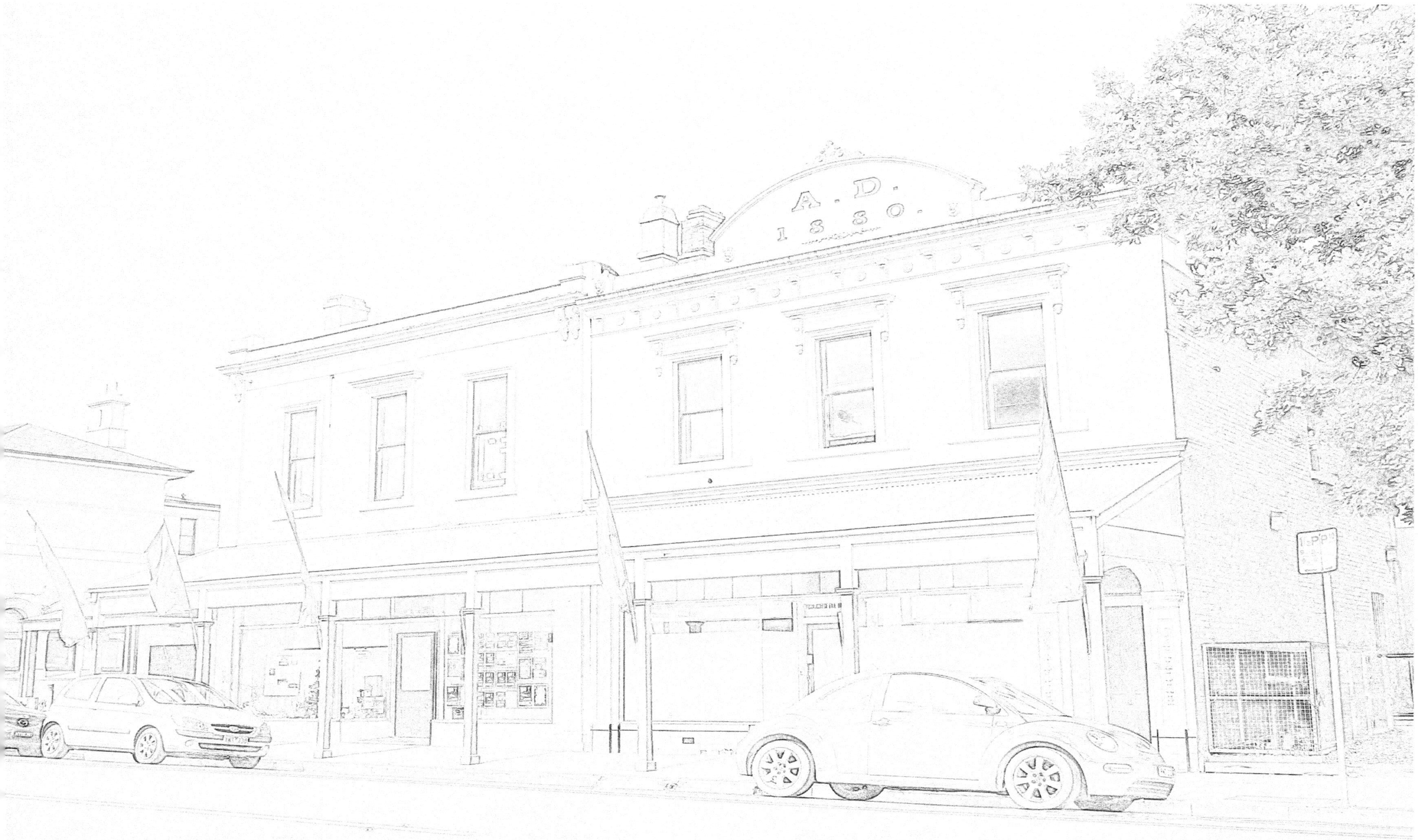
A.D.
1880

POST
KYNETON POST OFFICE
Civic Guide
GUIDE to KYNETON
nab

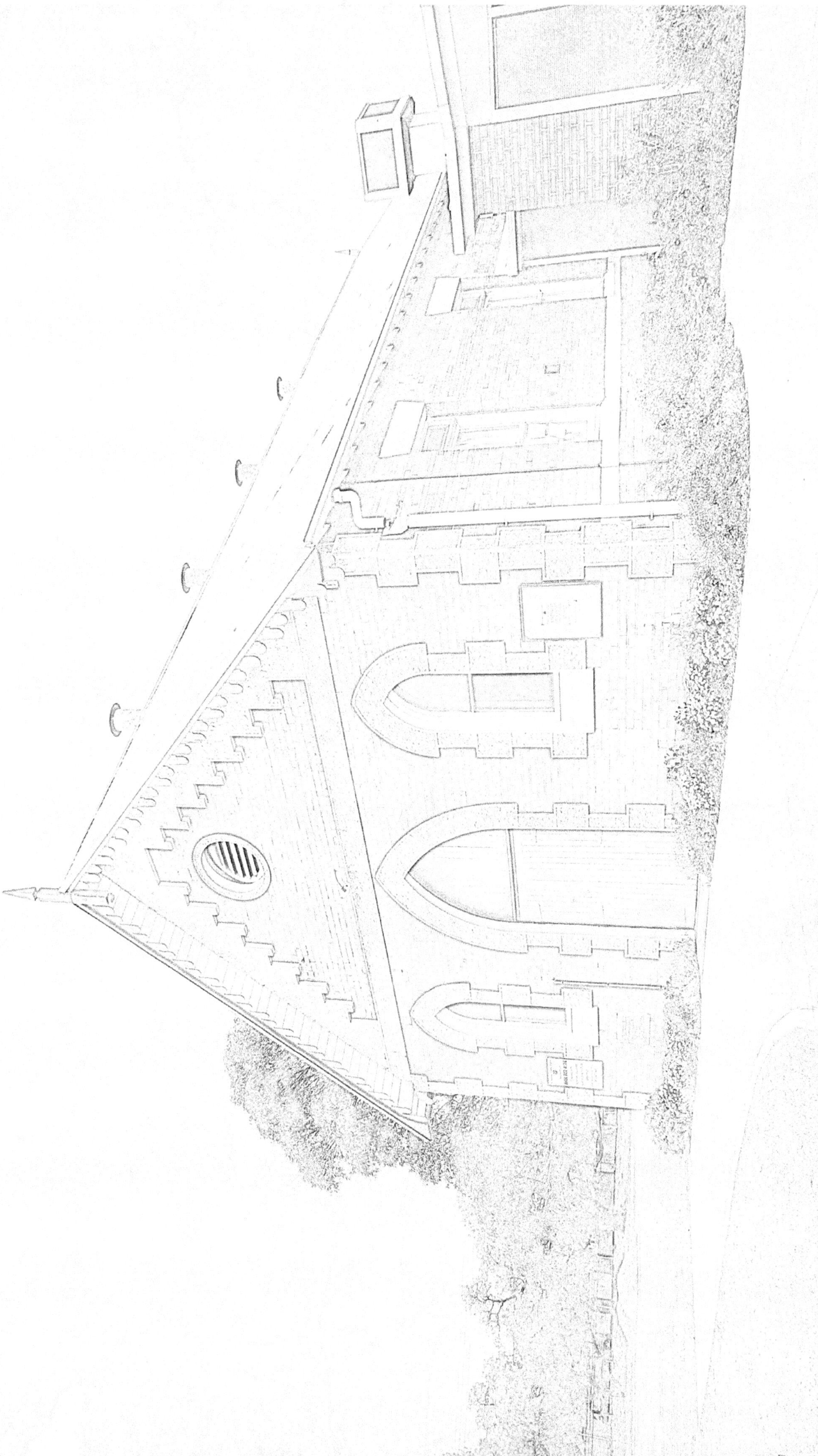

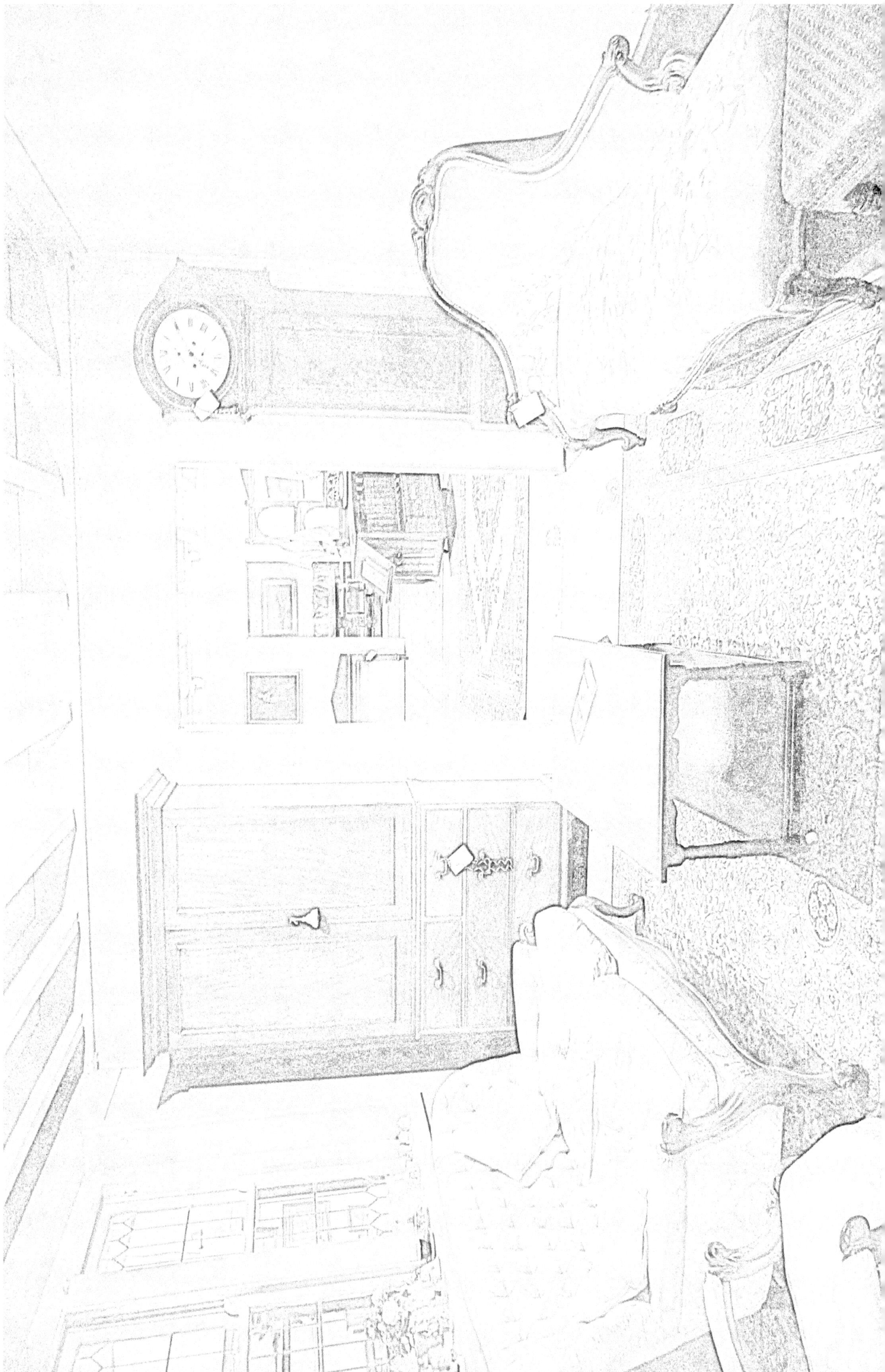

Big Guitar

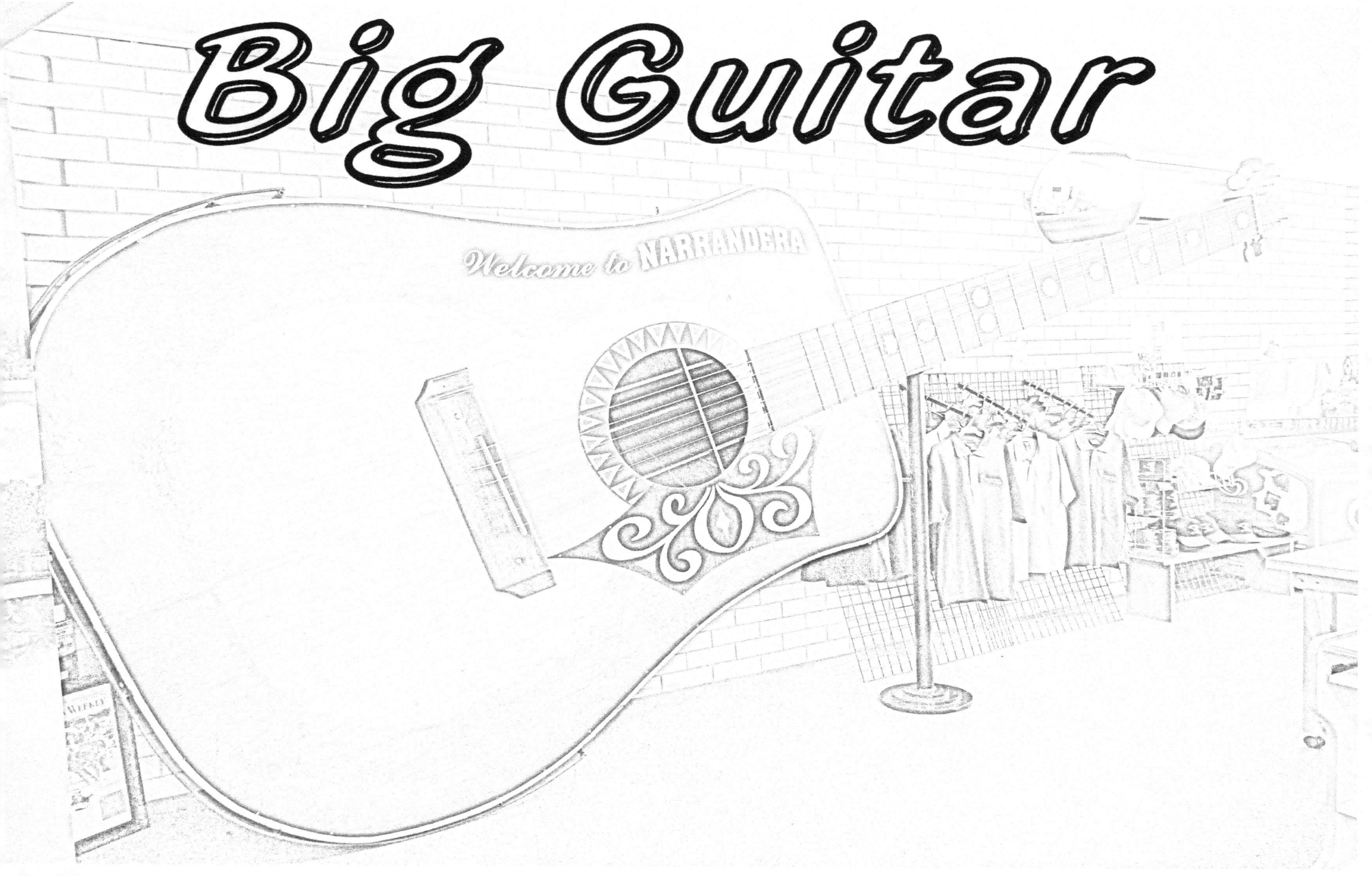

www.ingramcontent.com/pod-product-compliance
Lightning Source LLC
Chambersburg PA
CBHW081049180526
45170CB00005B/1744